THE MERCHANTS OF HARLEM

Volume 1, Sage Library of Social Research

SAGE LIBRARY OF SOCIAL RESEARCH

The Merchants of Harlem

A Study of Small Business in a Black Community

David Caplovitz

with the assistance of
Lois Sanders
Bernard Levenson
Joan Wilson

Volume 1
SAGE LIBRARY OF
SOCIAL RESEARCH

SAGE PUBLICATIONS   Beverly Hills   London

For information address:

SAGE PUBLICATIONS, INC.
275 South Beverly Drive
Beverly Hills, California 90212

SAGE PUBLICATIONS LTD
St George's House / 44 Hatton Garden
London ECIN 8ER

Printed in the United States of America

International Standard Book Number   0-8039-0319-7(C)
                                     0-8039-0148-8(P)
Library of Congress Catalog Card No.   72-84046

FIRST PRINTING

To Annie, Miles and Tommy:

Continuities in Dedications

TABLE OF CONTENTS

ACKNOWLEDGMENTS

As is customary in large scale social research, a number of people contributed to the research effort. The three listed on the title page of course made substantial contributions. Bernard Levenson helped me to design the study; Joan Wilson recruited and supervised the interviewers and took charge of the coding of the questionnaires; and Lois Sanders applied her programming skills to generating the various tables from the computer. In addition to these three colleagues, I would like to thank Eric Single and Fred Sherrow who pitched in as the deadline for the report approached by running tables and doing some analysis.

This research was carried out at Columbia University's Bureau of Applied Social Research. Mrs. Madeline Simonson and Ms. Phyllis Sheridan of the Bureau's supporting staff were extremely helpful in providing a variety of administrative services and it is a pleasure to thank them for their efforts.

−David Caplovitz
August 1973

INTRODUCTION

This survey of Harlem retail business was conducted as part of the research carried out by The Harlem Development Project at Columbia University on behalf of the Harlem Commonwealth Council, Inc., an organization that strives to stimulate black entrepreneurship and assist black businessmen with their problems. During the spring and summer of 1968, extensive interviews were conducted with a sample of businessmen in Central Harlem, an area bounded on the north by the Harlem River, on the west by St. Nicholas Avenue, on the east by Third Avenue, and on the south by 110th Street. In addition, we interviewed a control group of businessmen located in the Bay Ridge section of Brooklyn, a white, middle-class area. In all, 259 Harlem businessmen were interviewed, roughly 80 percent of the intended sample, and 53 businessmen were interviewed in Bay Ridge. Of the Harlem businessmen, 125 were blacks, 106 were whites, and 17 were Spanish-speaking. An additional 11 business establishments were owned by Orientals, racially mixed partners, or persons for whom race could not be determined. The Spanish-speaking owners and those in the heterogeneous group of 11 have been eliminated from the analysis. The report focuses on the black and white owners in Harlem and the control sample from Bay Ridge.

This report is essentially descriptive. The study was not designed to test hypotheses, but rather to permit a systematic comparison of black and white Harlem businessmen and to learn whether their differential experiences are due primarily to race or to other factors such as business experience, size, and type of establishment. The Bay Ridge control group allows us to compare merchants in a middle-class area with those in a black ghetto community. To what extent are the problems of Harlem businessmen, regardless of race, different from those of the merchants in a more affluent community? Does the locale of the business impose conditions that affect black and white owners equally—conditions that set them apart from the merchants in Bay Ridge? In short, throughout the analysis we shall be concerned with two types of comparisons, the blacks versus the whites in Harlem and the Harlem merchants versus those in Bay Ridge.

A Note on the Sample

The sample for this study was not designed to be precisely representative of the business establishments in Harlem. After consultation with the Harlem Commonwealth Council (HCC), it was decided to restrict the study to retail establishments, thus eliminating a number of wholesale and manufacturing firms to be found in Harlem. But even within the retail sector, the sample is not truly representative. HCC expressed an interest in certain categories of retailing which it had already decided were potential fields for investment and other types of economic action. These categories included grocery stores, drug stores, hardware stores, furniture and appliance stores, music stores, and the whole complex of automotive services. These store types were therefore designated for specific study. In addition, other specific store types were included on the basis of preliminary estimates of their relative importance in Harlem as measured by their annual gross sales. All other retail stores and service establishments that were believed to be too small to warrant recognition as a separate type were grouped into a miscellaneous category. The final set of categories consisted of 27 separate store types plus one miscellaneous category.

Names and addresses of stores were chosen from a file of New York City businesses furnished by the Finance Department of the City of New York. This file contained a "business code" for type of establishment which is similar to the U.S. Bureau of the Budget's Standard Industrial Classification.

Stores comprising the sample were randomly selected within each of the 28 types of stores located in the Central Harlem area. But, *a uniform proportion within each type was not selected.* Instead, those types that were believed to be most important for the overall purposes of the research project (that is, most important to the interests of HCC) were over-sampled to insure adequate results. Proportionately smaller numbers of stores were picked within the remaining types. For control purposes, a smaller sample of stores in the Bay Ridge area of Brooklyn was chosen by a similar process.

Our final sample is not truly representative of Harlem retail establishments. Certain categories were over- or under-sampled; not all sampled firms cooperated; and there was some turnover in the establishments at the sampled addresses. Thus we discovered that some businesses had closed down and no store was located at the address. In some instances, the sampled firm had moved and been replaced by a different type of business. Our rule was to interview the owner of the establishment at the sampled address even though the type of business might have changed.

Because of the unrepresentativeness of the sample, our distributions cannot be extrapolated to the entire Harlem community. For example, the fact that 48 percent of those interviewed were black owners, 41 percent white owners, 7 percent Spanish-speaking, and 4 percent Orientals and racially mixed owners, does not mean that this is the ethnic profile of Harlem businessmen.

Our main concern is comparing white and black business-men in the Harlem community, and even if one or the other group is over- or underrepresented, these comparisons are likely to be valid. Should we find, for example, that white-owned establishments in our sample are larger than those owned by blacks, this finding is likely to be true for the entire community. In short, it is most unlikely that a truly representative sample would change any of our findings concerning the *differences* between black- and white-owned establishments.

Chapter 1

TYPE AND STRUCTURE OF BLACK- AND

WHITE-OWNED BUSINESSES IN HARLEM

This chapter examines a number of the characteristics of the establishments owned by blacks and whites in Harlem and the merchants in Bay Ridge. We begin by showing the distribution of type of store in our three samples.

As can be seen from Table 1.1, proportionately more whites than blacks in Harlem own food, apparel, and home-furnishing stores and proportionately more blacks than whites own eating and drinking places and personal service establishments. The Bay Ridge sample is totally lacking in apparel stores and contains only a few establishments offering personal services. On the other hand, it contains proportionately more food and home-furnishing stores than either of the Harlem samples.

Type of store will be a critical factor in the subsequent analysis and because of the relatively small size of the samples, it is necessary to combine the types. The eight categories shown in Table 1.1 have been combined into four—two service categories and two in which products are sold. Automotive services remains as one service type, and the eating and drinking establishments have been grouped with personal services as the second service category. Stores that sell merchandise have been grouped according to whether they sell "low-cost" or "high-cost" items. By this criterion we have grouped food stores with those miscellaneous and general merchandise stores selling inexpensive items; and apparel, jewelry, automotive accessories, and home-furnishing stores as those that sell relatively expensive items.

The "combined" version of Table 1.1 is shown in Table 1.2.

The types of business establishments shown here make even clearer the differences between black- and white-owned retail establishments in Harlem. Fully a third of black-owned businesses provide services other than automotive, compared with less than one-fifth of the white-owned businesses in Harlem. In contrast, the white merchants in Harlem are much more likely than the blacks to be selling relatively costly merchandise (36 percent compared with 19 percent). The Bay Ridge merchants in our sample show up more frequently than both groups of Harlem merchants in the automotive services and in the low-dollar-item categories, and proportionately fewer are in the "other services" category (consisting of personal services and eating and drinking establishments).

Size of Establishment

However size is measured—by square feet of floor space, by number of employees, or by volume of annual sales—we find that white-owned businesses in Harlem tend to be larger than black-owned ones. Thus 67 percent of white owners have more than 1,000 square feet of floor space compared

TABLE 1.1
DISTRIBUTION OF TYPES OF BUSINESS
IN EACH OF THE THREE SAMPLES
(in percentages)

| Type of Business | Harlem Merchants | | Bay Ridge Merchants |
	Blacks	Whites	
Food stores	13	18	23
Apparel stores	4	16	—
Home furnishings (furniture; radio; TV; appliances)	10	16	28
General merchandise: Miscellaneous low-cost items (hardware; drugs; liquor; stationery)	25	21	25
Miscellaneous high-cost items (jewelry, auto supplies)	6	4	—
Auto services (gas stations; storage; rental)	10	8	17
Eating and Drinking Places	14	10	4
Personal services (laundry; barbershops; beauty shops; funeral parlors)	19	8	4
Total	101	101	101
n	(125)	(106)	(53)

TABLE 1.2
DISTRIBUTION OF MERCHANTS
ACCORDING TO TYPE OF STORE
(in percentages)

| Type of Business | Harlem Merchants | | Bay Ridge Merchants |
	Blacks	Whites	
Auto services	10	8	17
Other services	33	18	8
Low-cost items	38	39	47
High-cost items	19	36	28
Total	100	101	100
n	(126)	(106)	(53)

with 40 percent of black owners. It should be noted that these figures are based only on those in each group who could provide an answer about their amount of floor space. Almost one-third of the black owners did not have this information compared with less than one-tenth of the white owners. A similar pattern emerges when size is measured by number of employees. Only 41 percent of the black-owned businesses have at least two non-family employees (apart from the owner) in contrast with 76 percent of the white-owned businesses. About one-fifth of the black and white owners refused to answer the item about gross sales in 1967. But of those who did answer, we find that 51 percent of the white owners reported gross sales exceeding $100,000 compared with 16 percent of the black owners.

These three indicators of size have been combined into a size index that will be used frequently in the subsequent analysis. In constructing this measure, we took account of the frequent "no answers" by allocating firms to one of three size categories—small, medium, or large—on the basis of the information provided. Most respondents answered at least two of these questions and all but one answered at least one.

The distribution of the three samples according to size of establishment is shown in Table 1.3.

Table 1.3 merely confirms what we know from examining each indicator separately. The black merchants in Harlem are much more likely to own small establishments than are their white counterparts, and they are much less likely to own large establishments. More than three out of every five of the black merchants has a small establishment and only one in seven has a large one. In contrast, only about one in four of the white-owned businesses in Harlem is small and two out of every five are large. The Bay Ridge businesses fall between the Harlem blacks and whites on the dimension of size.

As size and type of establishment are important to the subsequent analysis, their relationship must be examined. Do the large retail establishments tend to be of one type, and

small establishments of another type, or are these characteristics independent of each other? Table 1.4 provides the
answer.

The auto service establishments are most likely to be large,
whereas establishments selling low-cost items are most likely
to be small. But the striking finding in Table 1.4 is that small,
medium, and large stores are quite prevalent in each type of
business. These two dimensions are thus largely independent
of each other.

Although there is no clear association between size and
type of business in the aggregate, striking differences do
appear when this relationship is examined within each ethnic
group. This can be seen from the two parts of Table 1.5, the
first part showing the frequency of *small* establishments in
each sample by type of store, and the second part showing
the frequency of *large* establishments. (The reader concerned
with the frequency of medium-sized establishments can
compute this from the data in both halves of the table.)

By comparing the first and second columns of Table 1.5A,
we learn that the differences in size between black- and
white-owned Harlem businesses cannot be explained by the
types of business they own. In every type of business, the
black-owned stores are much more likely to be small. This is
particularly true of the stores selling high-cost items. Most
black-owned stores selling relatively expensive merchandise
tend to be small (88 percent) in contrast with only 18
percent of the white-owned Harlem stores of this type.
Again, the Bay Ridge merchants tend to fall in the middle,
although none of the Bay Ridge auto service establishments is
small. Too much credence cannot be given to some of the
percentages in this table since the bases are quite small, but
the size differential between black- and white-owned businesses of every type is clearly significant. The black merchants of Harlem tend to have smaller enterprises than the
whites, whatever type of business they are in.

Table 1.5B shows the reverse in that it presents the
proportion in each sample with *large* establishments when
type of business is held constant.

TABLE 1.3
DISTRIBUTION OF BUSINESSMEN
ACCORDING TO SIZE OF ESTABLISHMENT
(in percentages)

| Size of Establishment | Harlem Merchants | | Bay Ridge |
	Blacks	Whites	Merchants
Small	62	27	49
Medium	24	32	28
Large	14	41	23
Total	100	100	100
n	(124)	(106)	(53)

TABLE 1.4
DISTRIBUTION OF ESTABLISHMENTS
BY SIZE AND TYPE (in percentages)

Size of Establishment	Auto Services	Other Services	Low-Cost Items	High-Cost Items
Small	27	42	54	48
Medium	37	27	31	21
Large	37	31	15	31
Total	101	100	100	100
n	(30)	(64)	(112)	(77)

TABLE 1.5A
PERCENTAGE OF SMALL ESTABLISHMENTS
BY TYPE OF ESTABLISHMENT

| | Harlem Merchants | | | | Bay Ridge | |
| | Blacks | | Whites | | Merchants | |
Type of Establishment	%	n	%	n	%	n
Automotive services	46	(13)	25	(8)	0	(9)
Other services	46	(41)	32	(19)	50	(4)
Low-cost items	67	(46)	34	(41)	60	(25)
High-cost items	88	(24)	18	(38)	60	(15)

TABLE 1.5B
PERCENTAGE OF LARGE ESTABLISHMENTS
BY TYPE OF ESTABLISHMENT

| | Harlem Merchants | | | | Bay Ridge | |
| | Blacks | | Whites | | Merchants | |
Type of Establishment	%	n	%	n	%	n
Automotive services	31	(13)	38	(8)	45	(9)
Other services	20	(41)	53	(19)	50	(4)
Low-cost items	11	(46)	24	(41)	8	(25)
High-cost items	—	(24)	53	(38)	27	(15)

TABLE 1.6
LOCATION OF WHITE- AND BLACK-OWNED
HARLEM BUSINESSES (in percentages)

| | Harlem Merchants | |
Location of Store	Blacks	Whites
125th Street	4	35
Major avenues (7th; 8th; Lenox)	75	45
Minor avenues (5th; Park; 3rd; 116th Street)	21	20
Total	100	100
n	(125)	(106)

Just as the black merchants in Harlem were likely to have small establishments, so we now see that they are less likely than their white counterparts to have large stores, regardless of type. Again, the greatest disparity occurs in the stores selling high-cost items. Only in the automotive services do the Harlem blacks come close to the Harlem whites with respect to size. And again, the Bay Ridge sample (where the percentages are most unreliable because of the small number of cases) appears to fall between the Harlem whites and blacks. The basic conclusion to be drawn from these tables is that the black merchants in Harlem operate much smaller establishments than the white merchants even when they enter those fields in which the whites predominate, such as stores selling high-cost merchandise. In the type of business in which blacks are more prevalent than whites—personal services—the white establishments still tend to be larger. Perhaps this reflects the fact that the white-owned businesses are older or that whites have greater access to credit and other elements that correlate with business success. Whether these conjectures have any merit will be considered later.

Rental and Location

The same percentage of white and black owners rent their stores (approximately 85 percent) rather than own the buildings in which they are located. Consistent with the greater size of their establishments, the white merchants pay substantially higher rents. Fully two-thirds of the white merchants, in contrast with only one-third of the blacks, pay rents exceeding $200 per month; some 42 percent of the Harlem whites but only 14 percent of the blacks pay rents exceeding $400 per month. The data show that this differential in rentals is a result of the white-owned establishments being at more choice locations. The heart of the business district in Harlem is 125th Street, the most prized location in the area. Next in desirability are the major avenues in the area that are heavily traveled. The less desirable locations are on the minor avenues and side streets.

As can be seen from Table 1.6, the white businessmen are much more likely to be found on 125th Street, whereas the majority of the black-owned stores are on the three major avenues, Seventh, Eighth, and Lenox.

The fact that white-owned stores are more likely to be on 125th Street might well be related to size differences. Table 1.7 shows that this is not the case. Even when blacks own stores in the same locations as whites, they have a smaller percentage of large establishments.

Ownership, Age, and Origin

The white-owned Harlem businesses are not only larger and situated in more choice locations but more complex in their ownership structure (Table 1.8).

The black businesses are owned predominantly by single persons whereas the white-owned businesses tend to be incorporated. Type of ownership no doubt relates to size of black- and white-owned businesses, although size does not fully explain the differences (Table 1.9).

In both ethnic groups, the majority of small stores are owned by a single person, although in this category the black stores are more likely to be incorporated. As size increases, form of ownership becomes more complex, especially among the whites. In the medium-size range and especially in the large category, the stores owned by whites are much more likely to be incorporated. (Of course, the business may be owned by a family or partnership; but by incorporating, the owner may realize certain tax advantages and limitations in liability.) As size increases, the proportion of partnerships increases among the blacks, but there is little difference in the proportion who elect to incorporate. Put another way, Table 1.9 shows that even in the large category, a majority of the black stores retain the simplest ownership form, whereas

TABLE 1.7
PERCENTAGE OF LARGE ESTABLISHMENTS
BY LOCATION AND ETHNICITY OF OWNER

| | Harlem Merchants | | | |
| | Blacks | | Whites | |
Location	%	n	%	n
125th Street	0	(5)	60	(37)
Major avenues	14	(94)	29	(48)
Minor avenues	16	(25)	33	(21)

TABLE 1.8
TYPE OF OWNERSHIP IN HARLEM SAMPLE
BY ETHNICITY (in percentages)

Type of Ownership	Blacks	Whites	Bay Ridge
Sole owner	72	43	72
Partnership	14	13	15
Corporation	14	44	13
Total	100	100	100
n	(124)	(105)	(53)

TABLE 1.9
TYPE OF OWNERSHIP IN HARLEM SAMPLE
BY ETHNICITY AND SIZE OF ESTABLISHMENT
(in percentages)

| | Size of Establishment | | | | | |
| | Small | | Medium | | Large | |
Type of Ownership	Blacks	Whites	Blacks	Whites	Blacks	Whites
Sole owner	82	79	57	44	53	19
Partnership	7	18	23	9	29	14
Corporation	12	4	20	47	18	67
Total	101	101	100	100	100	100
n	(76)	(28)	(30)	(34)	(17)	(43)

the great majority of the white stores in this class are incorporated. To the extent that the corporate structure yields advantages, whites are more likely than blacks to have these benefits.

The white-owned establishments in Harlem also tend to be older than the black ones. Fifty-nine percent of the white-owned businesses, compared with 41 percent of the black-owned businesses, have been at the same address for 10 years or more. Moreover, the white establishments represent greater continuity than black ones. White owners were more likely to have had the same business at some previous location (54 percent versus 33 percent). On the average, the white owners have been in business both in Harlem and in the city for a substantially longer time.

Length of time in business might explain why the white-owned businesses are larger. Presumably, as a business becomes established, it grows in size. The black-owned businesses might be smaller because the owners have only recently entered the world of small business. But this interpretation also fails the empirical test. When owners are classified by the length of time they have been in business (Table 1.10), we find that whatever the length of time, the difference in size between black- and white-owned businesses persists.

By reading down the columns, we learn that the expected relationship between business experience and size of firm does not hold among the Harlem whites and the Bay Ridge merchants. Among Harlem blacks there is a hint that experience is related to firm size; the owners with less than 10 years' experience are much less likely to have large firms. If firms grow with experience, then it would appear that the first 10 years are the most crucial for expansion.

By reading across the rows of the table, we learn that the white owners' greater experience in business in no way explains their larger establishments, for within each level of experience Harlem whites are two or three times as likely as Harlem blacks to have large firms. Put another way, the barriers to expansion of black-owned businesses are more complicated than merely experience in business. Black merchants with more than 20 years' experience have only half the chance of owning a large establishment than white merchants with less than 10 years' experience.

Another factor that might account for the difference in the size of black- and white-owned businesses is the circumstances under which the business was started. The merchants were asked whether they themselves had started the business, bought it from someone else or inherited it. The man who inherits an ongoing business or has sufficient capital to buy out another businessman presumably has a head start on the one who must build his own. This issue of business origin also shows differences between the Harlem blacks and whites. Fully two-thirds of the black-owned businesses were started by the current owner compared with half the white-owned businesses. Thirty-eight percent of the whites said they had bought the business from the previous owner compared with 28 percent of the blacks; only 9 percent of the whites and 5 percent of the blacks inherited their businesses.

Whether the origin of the business sheds light on the marked difference in the size of the black- and white-owned businesses is shown in Table 1.11.

In neither group do we find any clear relationship between origin and current size. The seemingly greater proportion of large stores among the blacks who inherited their business must be discounted because the percentage is based on six cases. In both groups, self-started businesses are larger than those which were purchased from the previous owner.

Still another indicator of the greater complexity and success of the white-owned firms in Harlem is the fact that the whites are more likely than the blacks to own multiple stores. Twenty-three percent of the white businessmen own multiple units compared with 10 percent of the blacks. The difference is even greater than the percentages suggest, for the white who owns more than one store is apt to own several, whereas almost all of the blacks in the multiple-

TABLE 1.10
PERCENTAGE OF LARGE ESTABLISHMENTS BY LENGTH OF TIME IN BUSINESS AND ETHNICITY OF OWNERS

Length of Time in Business	Harlem Merchants				Bay Ridge Merchants	
	Blacks		Whites			
	%	n	%	n	%	n
Under 10 years	5	(44)	44	(23)	20	(15)
10-19 years	15	(34)	40	(35)	27	(11)
20-29 years	20	(25)	36	(22)	25	(13)
30 years and over	18	(17)	44	(34)	25	(12)

TABLE 1.11
PERCENTAGE OF LARGE ESTABLISHMENTS, BY ETHNICITY OF OWNER AND ORIGINS OF BUSINESS (HARLEM)

Origins of Business	Harlem Merchants			
	Blacks		Whites	
	%	n	%	n
Owner-started business	15	(82)	49	(51)
Business purchased from previous owner	9	(35)	32	(41)
Inherited business	33	(6)	42	(12)

ownership category have only one other store. (Two black businessmen own three stores whereas 10 white businessmen in the sample own a minimum of three.)

Summary

Black businessmen in Harlem tend to own stores offering services, whereas the whites in Harlem own stores selling relatively high-cost merchandise. The white-owned establishments tend to be larger than those owned by blacks—whether measured by number of employees, number of square feet, or volume of gross sales. This difference in size cannot be explained by the difference in type of business, for within each type the white-owned stores are larger. The white owners pay higher rentals and in return command choice locations. White owners also have been in business longer, their establishments are older, and more likely to be incorporated. White owners are also more likely to have bought out an ongoing business rather than to have started a new one.

These differences in the structure of white- and black-owned firms do not explain why the white-owned establishments are larger. When location, age of establishment, type of ownership, and origins of the business are held constant, the white-owned businesses remain larger than those owned by blacks. It is possible that a multivariate analysis would enable us to explain some of the differences in the size of the firms, but the persistence of a substantial difference in size when each factor was examined individually suggests that the explanation must be sought elsewhere.

To some extent these findings reflect the history of Harlem. During the past fifty years, it has changed from a white middle-class area to a Negro ghetto. And in part, these findings reflect the relative newness of blacks to the world of small business with the attendant problems of capitalization and business experience. The concentration of black businesses in the service sectors is in keeping with newness to business life. Such businesses demand a lot of labor and little capitalization and serve as points of entry into private enterprise. The inability of the analysis to explain the size differential between black- and white-owned businesses, however, suggests that the black businessmen face handicaps that transcend the succession of one ethnic group by another in the economic arena.

Chapter 2

A PROFILE OF BLACK AND WHITE BUSINESSMEN

Having compared the type and structure of businesses owned by black and white merchants in Harlem, we turn to an examination of the businessmen themselves. How do black and white businessmen compare with respect to business experience, participation in a business culture, and social origins?

The data indicate that the white businessmen generally have had more experience in the world of business and have been immersed in a business culture, in keeping with the succession model of blacks being the newcomers replacing the older immigrant groups in the community (Gans, 1969).

White owners tend to be older than blacks. The median ages for our three samples are as follows:

Bay Ridge merchants . . . . 44.3 years
Black merchants in Harlem . . . . 49.2 years
White merchants in Harlem . . . . 52.3 years

The differences in ages between white and black merchants in Harlem account for little of the disparity in business experience. For example, 54 percent of the whites compared with 36 percent of the blacks have been in business for 20 or more years. At the other extreme, 35 percent of the blacks have had less than 10 years of business experience compared with 22 percent of the whites. Whites were also more likely than blacks to have owned some other business prior to their present one (41 percent compared with 28 percent). Even these figures do not fully reflect the head start of the white businessmen. Considering those in each group who had *not* been in business for themselves but had worked for someone else, we find that 44 percent of the whites in this category had managerial or sales experience compared with only 16 percent of the blacks. Previous research has shown that blue-collar workers often aspire to owning their own businesses. Black owners, more than the white owners, bear this out (Chinoy, 1952). Thus 65 percent of the blacks who started their occupational careers by working for someone else had held blue-collar jobs compared with 4 percent of the whites.

White businessmen are more likely than black businessmen to come from the middle class. Fifty-seven percent of the Harlem whites compared with 21 percent of the blacks were sons of white-collar workers. This difference is due to the preponderance of salesmen among the fathers of the white businessmen (36 versus 6 percent), one further indication of the whites' greater exposure to business culture.

Class differences are also reflected in the stability of family life. Ninety percent of the Harlem whites compared with 62 percent of the blacks are currently married. The blacks are more likely than the whites to be widowed, separated or divorced.

A strong indication of the different financial circumstances of the black and white merchants is the number of working wives. Fifty-nine percent of the currently married blacks have working wives; the corresponding figure for whites is 15 percent. This could stem from the greater need for the spouse to assist the black owner in running his business, but it could also reflect the need for additional family income.

In keeping with their higher socio-economic origins, the white businessmen of Harlem had more education than their black counterparts. Seventy-five percent of the whites as compared with 48 percent of the blacks were at least high school graduates and 42 percent of the whites compared with 22 percent of the blacks had at least some college education.

The literature on occupational choice places great emphasis on the "role model," that is, a personal acquaintance who by his own example influences the career decision of the individual. This survey makes quite clear that the white businessmen were much more likely than the black businessmen to have role models. Sixty-nine percent of the whites compared with 39 percent of the blacks reported that they had close relatives in business.

That white businessmen are more likely than the blacks to come from a business culture suggests different patterns of recruitment to business. The white owner is apt to assimilate the culture of business through personal relationships. This occurs less frequently for blacks, who must rely more on formal institutions for their knowledge of business. When asked whether they had taken courses to prepare for business, more blacks answered affirmatively (35 percent) than whites (26 percent).

Two questions asked of the merchants measure their involvement in the business community: (1) whether they subscribe to or read trade publications, and (2) whether they belong to any trade associations. No difference between blacks and whites appears on the first measure as 54 percent of each group regularly read trade publications. But the whites were twice as likely to belong to trade associations as the blacks (51 versus 24 percent). This undoubtedly reflects the greater involvement of the whites in the more prestigious locations of Harlem, such as 125th Street.

In order to explore their motivation for going into business, the merchants were asked their reasons for choosing this type of occupation. A most revealing difference emerges in response to this open-ended question as can be seen from Table 2.1.

Earlier we saw that somewhat larger percentages of blacks and whites actually inherited their business than is shown in this table. This table deals with motivations for going into business rather than objective circumstances. The striking difference occurs in the two categories of desiring independence and desiring financial success. Being one's own boss has much stronger appeal to the black than to the white businessmen. In contrast, whites are much more likely to regard business as an avenue to economic mobility. It is tempting to interpret these differences as indicating that blacks turn to business in order to avoid exploitation. The reasons of the merchants in the control group, oddly enough, appear to be more similar to those of the Harlem blacks than to those of the Harlem whites.

To conclude this portrait of the black and white Harlem businessmen, we note some demographic differences in the two groups. A larger percentage of the whites were born in New York City (42 percent contrasted with 10 percent of the blacks); more than half the blacks were born in the South (56 percent). It has often been observed that blacks raised in the Caribbean have greater contact with business and a stronger spirit of self-reliance than native blacks. Since we do not know what proportion of the New York black population comes from the West Indies, we have no idea whether West Indians are overrepresented in our sample, but we can report that 14 percent of the blacks were born in the Caribbean. This is the largest group after the Southern-born.

Business Background and Size of Establishment

We have seen that the white businessmen in Harlem have had more business experience than the blacks and are also more likely to have come from a business culture. Do these facts in any way explain why they have larger enterprises? The white businessmen were almost twice as likely to have had a close relative in business, a person who might well have assisted them in starting their business. Table 2.2 explores the possible impact of a relative in business on size of establishment. Again, we shall show the distribution of both small and large businesses according to these variables.

Table 2.2 shows that having a relative in business is related to size of establishment for the Harlem whites, to some extent for the Bay Ridge merchants, but not at all for the blacks. In fact, the blacks who do not have relatives in business are slightly more likely than those who do to own large establishments.

Much has been written about the shortcomings of the Negro family. The thesis has been presented by Moynihan and others that a major obstacle to success of American blacks is the relative instability in the basic family unit. Table 2.2 might point to a somewhat different conclusion. Even when the black family can provide role models, training, and support, the barriers to "success" are apparently so great that blacks do not benefit as much as whites from the extended family. It is possible that the businessmen-relatives of the blacks in our sample, like themselves, owned predominantly small marginal businesses and hence could not offer as much help as the businessmen-relatives of our two samples of whites.

We have combined into an index of business background some of the items presented above, namely, relatives in business, years of business experience, having had business courses, regular reading of a trade journal, and belonging to a trade association. Table 2.3 summarizes the earlier finding: the black businessmen of Harlem have much less of a business background than either the Harlem whites or the businessmen in Bay Ridge.

The Bay Ridge merchants turn out to have the strongest business background as two-thirds of them score high on this

TABLE 2.1
REASONS FOR GOING INTO BUSINESS (in percentages)

Reasons	Harlem Merchants		Bay Ridge Merchants
	Blacks	Whites	
Inherited business	2	7	7
Difficulty finding employment	3	2	11
Desire to be own boss	41	13	37
Desire to have own business	9	4	11
Desire to improve financial status	43	73	35
Service needed in community	3	—	—
Total	101	99	101
n	(111)	(99)	(46)
Irrelevant comment; No answer	11	7	10
n	(125)	(106)	(53)

TABLE 2.2
SIZE OF BUSINESS ACCORDING TO WHETHER OWNER
HAS A CLOSE RELATIVE IN BUSINESS (in percentages)

	n	% Owning Small Stores	% Owning Large Stores
Harlem Blacks			
Relative in business	(47)	62	8
No relative in business	(73)	62	16
Harlem Whites			
Relative in business	(72)	21	44
No relative in business	(32)	41	32
Bay Ridge			
Relative in business	(42)	45	24
No relative in business	(10)	60	20

TABLE 2.3

DISTRIBUTION OF MERCHANTS ACCORDING TO
INDEX OF BUSINESS BACKGROUND (in percentages)

Business Background Index	Harlem Merchants		Bay Ridge Merchants
	Blacks	Whites	
Low	48	25	11
Medium	17	22	23
High	34	54	66
Total	99	101	100
n	(122)	(106)	(53)

TABLE 2.4

SIZE OF ESTABLISHMENT BY BUSINESS
BACKGROUND INDEX (in percentages)

	n	% Owning Small Stores	% Owning Large Stores
Harlem Black Merchants			
BBI Low[a]	(58)	69	10
BBI Medium	(21)	62	9
BBI High	(42)	52	19
Harlem White Merchants			
BBI Low	(26)	62	23
BBI Medium	(23)	22	43
BBI High	(57)	14	47
Bay Ridge Merchants			
BBI Low	(6)	67	17
BBI Medium	(12)	58	17
BBI High	(35)	43	26

a. BBI refers to the Business Background Index.

index. More than half the white Harlem merchants but only one-third of the black businessmen score high. Whether strength of business background in any way explains the white merchants of Harlem having larger enterprises can be seen from Table 2.4, which shows the percentages of small and large firms in each sample according to business background.

Table 2.4 shows that degree of business experience is indeed related to size of establishment within each of the three samples. Despite the small base figures in the Bay Ridge sample, this group also shows the relationship. In each sample, the stronger the business background, the less likely is the businessman to have a small establishment and the more likely he is to have a large one. The connection between experience in the world of business and size of establishment is particularly strong among the whites of Harlem. The relationship is weakest among blacks as those with substantial business experience are only slightly more likely to have large establishments than those with little business background. In this respect the Bay Ridge merchants fall between the whites and blacks of Harlem. Although they are most likely to have substantial business experience, this type of background does not automatically insure them of a large enterprise. Table 2.4 shows the connection between business experience and size of establishment within each of the three samples, but by comparing comparable columns across the three samples we learn that the Harlem blacks benefit least from business experience. Of those who have little experience, only 10 percent of the blacks have large establishments in contrast with 23 percent of the Harlem whites and 17 percent of the Bay Ridge whites. The disparity is more evident when we consider those who have been immersed in a business culture. Among the Harlem blacks with such a background, only 19 percent have large firms, in contrast with 26 percent of the Bay Ridge whites and 47 percent of the Harlem whites. To be highly sophisticated in the world of business has a much bigger pay-off for the Harlem whites. This finding is reminiscent of the numerous studies which have shown that formal education has a lower pay-off for blacks than for whites. Department of Labor studies have shown that black high school graduates earn less than white high school drop-outs. We have chosen to interpret Table 2.4 as showing the effect of business experience on size of establishment. But it should be noted that the causal relationship could go in the other direction. Some of the items that went into the index of business background clearly seem prior to size of firm, such as having close relatives in business, having taken business courses, and years of business experience. But others, such as reading trade journals regularly and belonging to trade associations, might well be consequences of business success. In short, it is possible, although not probable, that Table 2.4 indicates that the more successful businessmen (judged by size of establishment) are more likely to be immersed in a business culture. But since the balance of indicators that comprise the index are determined prior to size of firm, it seems more likely that business background is a factor accounting for size. If so, then the obstacles confronting black businessmen are evident. Just as the black high school graduate fails to do as well as the white high school drop-out, so the black with extensive business experience fails to do as well as the white with less experience. This thesis is based on the equating of size of firm with success. When we consider the profitability of the business, we shall confront this question directly.

Residence of Harlem Businessmen

The charge has often been made that the businesses in black ghetto areas tend to be owned by whites who live outside the community and thus take money out of the area. Since our sample is not completely representative of Harlem retail establishments, we do not know what proportion of such businesses are owned by whites, but we do know where the black and white businessmen in our sample live. On the basis of these data, it is quite clear that the whites do not live in Harlem, whereas a majority of the black businessmen do (Table 2.5).

Only 2 percent of the white businessmen live in Harlem. The majority of whites live elsewhere in the city and more than one-third of them live in the suburbs. While the majority of blacks live in Harlem, 41 percent do not. Roughly, therefore, if all businesses in Harlem were black-owned, the number of merchants who lived in the community would increase by about 27 percent.[1] The flight to the suburbs and more desirable dwelling places is not exclusively a white phenomenon. As the racial barriers in the suburbs break down under the impetus of open housing legislation, increasing numbers of black businessmen will undoubtedly move out of the ghetto.

That the desirability of the area, independent of the racial match between businessman and the community he serves, is important in determining the residence of the merchant is suggested by the strikingly different pattern in the control group. Fully 85 percent of the Bay Ridge merchants live in Brooklyn, a figure much higher than the proportion of blacks living in Harlem (59 percent) or living in the borough of Manhattan (70 percent), an area more comparable to Brooklyn than is Harlem. This finding suggests that the relationship between the black businessman and the black community depends as much on social class as on race. Whether the trend toward black entrepreneurship in Harlem will result in more businessmen living in the community would seem to depend on whether Harlem can shift from a low-income to a middle-income community.

We can test this theory by examining the connection between size of establishment—our crude measure of business success—and place of residence of the black merchants in the sample (Table 2.6).

Table 2.6 confirms our expectations. As black businessmen become more successful, they are more likely to live outside Harlem. Two-thirds of the black owners of small stores but

TABLE 2.5
RESIDENCE OF BLACK AND WHITE
HARLEM BUSINESSMEN (in percentages)

Location of Residence	Blacks	Whites
Harlem	59	2
Elsewhere in New York City	28	60
Suburbs	12	37
Total	99	99
n	(123)	(106)

TABLE 2.6
RESIDENCE OF BLACK HARLEM MERCHANTS ACCORDING
TO SIZE OF ESTABLISHMENT (in percentages)

Place of Residence	Size of Black-Owned Establishments		
	Small	Medium	Large
Harlem	67	53	31
Elsewhere in New York City	32	33	44
Suburbs	1	13	25
Total	100	99	100
n	(76)	(30)	(16)

TABLE 2.7
PERCENTAGE APPROVING OF BUSINESS CAREER FOR
THEIR CHILDREN, BY SIZE OF ESTABLISHMENT[a]

	Harlem Merchants				Bay Ridge Merchants	
	Blacks		Whites			
Size of Establishment	%	n	%	n	%	n
Small	70	(47)	62	(21)	60	(20)
Medium	68	(22)	40	(30)	46	(11)
Large	83	(12)	50	(36)	38	(8)

a. The base figures in this table are limited to those businessmen who have children.

less than one-third of the owners of large stores live in Harlem. The data also confirm the attraction of the suburbs to the more successful black merchants: virtually no small store owners live in the suburbs but 25 percent of those owning large stores do. It would seem that only the transformation of Harlem from a low-income community to one which can easily accommodate middle-class families can stem this tide, especially with the breakdown of the barriers to suburban living that have confronted the blacks in the past.

In closing, we have one item that indirectly reveals the attitude of black and white businessmen toward business as a career. The merchants who had been married were asked whether they had children and, if so, whether they would approve, disapprove, or not care if their children selected business as a career. The difference in responses between the black and white merchants is striking. Fully 72 percent of the blacks approve of their children selecting a business career, compared with only 48 percent of the Harlem whites. No doubt this difference reflects the different stages of social mobility of black and white businessmen. Small business was often pursued as an avenue of social mobility by America's immigrant groups in the early twentieth century. The children of these businessmen now tend to seek still higher social status by pursuing professional careers. That black businessmen are much more likely to approve of business as a career for their children would suggest that they are at an earlier stage in the struggle for social mobility. This inference finds support when we relate size of establishment to approval of a business career for children (Table 2.7).

Perhaps the first thing to be noted in Table 2.7 is that the blacks more than the whites and the merchants in the control group approve a business career on each size level. Secondly, there is some tendency for approval among the blacks to be positively related to size of establishment, suggesting that blacks who have "made it" in business are especially likely to take a positive view toward a business career. They may also have a profitable business to transmit to their children. But among Harlem whites, where the pattern is more irregular, it would seem that large owners are not as eager as the small ones to have their children follow in their footsteps. Presumably they have still higher aspirations for their children. This is especially true of the merchants in the Bay Ridge sample. There we find that approval of a business career for one's children steadily declines with increase in size. This result tends to support the inference that black businessmen are at an earlier stage in the process of social mobility.

Summary

White merchants of Harlem have substantially more experience in the world of business than their black counterparts. Furthermore, for whites, the experience is more correlated with success (as measured by size of firm) than it is for the blacks. The few blacks who seem to have been immersed in a business culture are less likely than whites to own large firms. This finding suggests yet another form of inequality in the American opportunity structure confronting blacks and whites, one which yields differential rewards for education.

Chapter 3

BUSINESS PRACTICES

The businessmen in our sample were asked a number of questions about their business practices covering such matters as the racial composition of their work force and clientele, the length of time their stores remain open, their promotion practices, their credit practices, their methods of taking inventory, and the frequency with which they have financial statements prepared.

Employees and Customers

We have already seen that whites were much more likely than blacks to have non-family employees. Even though fewer white than black businessmen were interviewed, the latter had a total of 44 employees (other than family members) compared with 237 for the white businessmen. Table 3.1 shows the racial composition of their work forces.

Not surprisingly, virtually all employees of the black businessmen are black. But Table 3.1 shows that three out of every five of the employees of white merchants are black. In addition, the white merchants are more likely than blacks to hire Spanish-speaking employees, presumably to cater to the increasing number of Spanish-speaking residents of Harlem.

Differences in the composition of the work force of black and white Harlem businessmen are related to the racial composition of their customers. Seventy-five percent of the blacks report that at least 90 percent of their customers are black, compared with 64 percent of the whites. White and black businessmen report similarly small proportions of white customers, the difference being that white businessmen cater to Spanish-speaking customers more often than their black counterparts (19 percent of the whites compared with only 6 percent of the blacks report that at least 20 percent of their customers are Spanish-speaking).

Apart from the racial composition of their customers, the merchants were asked the proportion of their customers living in Harlem. Again we find a slight difference between Harlem black and white merchants. Some 82 percent of the blacks reported that most of their customers were local residents in contrast with 74 percent of the whites. The greater tendency of blacks to deal mainly with Harlem residents can be explained partly by the differences in types of businesses that whites and blacks conduct, and partly by store location. Table 3.2 shows the proportion of black and white owners who report that most of their customers live in Harlem according to type of business.

In two types of business—other services and low-cost items—there is no difference between blacks and whites with respect to where their customers live. The greatest difference appears for automotive services but the calculation for whites in this category is based on only a few cases. The only substantial difference appears among merchants selling high-cost items. In this category, blacks are more likely than whites to deal with a local trade.

The relationship between store location and percentage of customers who reside in the area is exhibited in Table 3.3.

TABLE 3.1
RACIAL COMPOSITION OF EMPLOYEES OF
HARLEM MERCHANTS (in percentages)

Composition of Work Force	Blacks	Whites
Black	90	60
Spanish-speaking	5	17
White	5	23
Total	100	100
n	(44)	(237)

TABLE 3.2
HARLEM MERCHANTS WHO SAY THAT MOST OF
THEIR CUSTOMERS LIVE IN HARLEM, BY TYPE
OF BUSINESS AND ETHNICITY

| | Harlem Merchants | | | |
| | Blacks | | Whites | |
Type of Business	%	n	%	n
Automotive services	77	(13)	50	(8)
Other services	83	(41)	82	(17)
Low-cost items	87	(45)	90	(39)
High-cost items	78	(23)	61	(38)

TABLE 3.3
HARLEM MERCHANTS WHO SAY THAT MOST OF
THEIR CUSTOMERS LIVE IN HARLEM, BY
LOCATION OF STORE AND ETHNICITY

| | Harlem Merchants | | | |
| | Blacks | | Whites | |
Location of Store	%	n	%	n
125th Street	80	(5)	64	(36)
Major avenues	82	(91)	87	(45)
Minor avenues and 116th Street	85	(26)	67	(21)

Table 3.3 shows that the white owners located on 125th Street and on the minor avenues are less likely than black owners to cater to local residents, but the whites located on the major avenues of Harlem are slightly more likely than their black counterparts to cater to local residents. Thus the aggregate difference between blacks and whites is dependent, in part, on the location of the store.

It has been found in other studies that the low-income merchant is likely to experience a quasi-personal relationship with his customers, partly to control his credit customers and partly because the storekeeper in low-income areas is often cast in an advisor role by his customers on problems unrelated to his business (see, e.g., Caplovitz, 1963; Koos, 1946). Of course, how well a businessman knows his customers is likely to depend upon the length of time he has been in business and the type of merchandise he sells. Although blacks have not, on the average, been in business as long as whites, they are somewhat more likely to know their customers by name. Fifty-two percent of the blacks compared with 40 percent of the whites know at least half their customers by name. The Bay Ridge merchants are even more likely to know their customers; fully two-thirds of them report knowing at least one-half by name. The difference between blacks and whites in Harlem suggests that the blacks are somewhat better integrated into the community. Curiously, the age of the establishment is unrelated to the owners knowing their customers (Table 3.4).

Longevity alone is clearly not the source of familiarity. Other factors, such as type of business, are, no doubt, important.

Services to Customers: Store Hours,
Credit, and Other Services

We have seen that black-owned stores are generally smaller than those owned by whites. It also turns out that the black owners work longer than the Harlem whites, since they keep their stores open more hours per week and are more likely than the whites to remain open every day of the week. Thus 36 percent of the black businessmen, compared with 19 percent of the Harlem whites, report that their stores are open seven days a week; and whereas 29 percent of the white-owned businesses are open less than 60 hours a week, this is true of only 10 percent of the black-owned businesses. At the other extreme, 65 percent of the blacks compared with 42 percent of the whites keep their stores open more than 70 hours a week. These differences cannot be explained by size of firm, for as the rows of Table 3.5 show, on every size level black-owned stores are open, on the average, more hours than the white-owned stores. Among black-owned stores, hours open per week increase with size, but this is not true of the Harlem whites nor those in the control group.

How long a store remains open, of course, is related to the merchandise sold. The automotive stores (primarily gas stations) remain open the longest. All but one of the 30 stores in this category are open at least 70 hours a week; most of them remain open about 140 hours. The average for these stores is 136 hours per week. A distant second are the Other Services stores which, on the average, remain open 96 hours per week. The stores selling low-cost items are open an average of 84 hours, and the high-cost item stores remain open, on the average, about 65 hours, the shortest work-week.[2] We have seen that black-owned stores stay open longer even when size is held constant. Does this also hold when type of store is held constant? The answer is provided in Table 3.6.

The aggregate relationship between hours open and type of business holds in each of the three samples with one reversal among Bay Ridge merchants. In that sample, stores merchandising low-cost items tend to be open longer than Other Service stores. More important is the pattern exhibited in the

TABLE 3.4
PERCENTAGE IN EACH SAMPLE WHO KNOW AT LEAST HALF THEIR CUSTOMERS BY NAME, BY TIME AT CURRENT LOCATION

| | Harlem Merchants | | | | Bay Ridge Merchants | |
| | Blacks | | Whites | | | |
Years at Location	%	n	%	n	%	n
Under three	54	(35)	43	(23)	56	(16)
Three to ten	55	(33)	21	(19)	73	(11)
Ten or more	49	(43)	44	(56)	69	(23)

TABLE 3.5
MEAN NUMBER OF HOURS OPEN PER WEEK BY SIZE OF ESTABLISHMENT

| | Harlem Merchants | | | | Bay Ridge Merchants | |
| | Blacks | | Whites | | | |
Size of Establishment	%	n	%	n	%	n
Small	92	(76)	74	(29)	77	(25)
Medium	96	(29)	83	(34)	84	(14)
Large	125	(17)	80	(43)	84	(12)

TABLE 3.6
MEAN NUMBER OF HOURS OPEN PER WEEK EACH SAMPLE BY TYPE OF ESTABLISHMENT

| | Harlem Merchants | | | | Bay Ridge Merchants | |
| | Blacks | | Whites | | | |
Type of Business	%	n	%	n	%	n
Automotive services	154	(13)	136	(8)	110	(9)
Other services	100	(41)	95	(19)	68	(4)
Low-cost items	89	(45)	81	(41)	78	(24)
High-cost items	76	(24)	60	(38)	62	(14)

rows of Table 3.6. For each type of store, those owned by blacks tend to be open longer than those owned by Harlem whites, and the merchants in the control group tend to have the shortest hours (except in the high-cost-item categories where their average is slightly higher than that of the Harlem whites). The import of Tables 3.5 and 3.6 is that regardless of size or type of establishment, the black businessman puts in a longer week than his white counterpart. Whether this greater effort is required to compensate for handicaps confronting him or results in greater profits will be explored later.

Credit is generally regarded as an important part of the economic life of low-income areas. The poor consumer needs credit not only to make major purchases, but he also needs it from the corner grocer to tide him over until pay-day or until the welfare check comes. Many merchants in such areas evidently find it necessary to extend credit in order to stay in business. It is somwhat surprising, therefore, that three of every five Harlem merchants interviewed reported that they do not extend credit.

We know that the black merchants are more likely to own service-type establishments and that white businessmen are more likely to own businesses selling relatively expensive merchandise. These facts may explain why more whites extend credit. Table 3.7 shows the percentage of white and black merchants who currently extend credit, who used to but no longer do, and those who never extended credit.

From the first row of Table 3.7 we learn that more than one-half of the white merchants offer credit contrasted with only about one-third of the black merchants. This is not entirely accounted for by the different types of business, for as we can see from the second row, blacks were much more likely than whites to have offered credit in the past. When asked why they used to extend credit but no longer do, the most frequent explanation was that it resulted in excessive loss of money. One inference from this is that white merchants are more successful in managing their credit extensions perhaps because they have greater resources to absorb losses, or because they are better able to determine credit risks and control their credit customers.

The connection between extending credit and type of business is shown in Table 3.8.

In every group, the automotive service establishments are most likely to offer credit, reflecting no doubt the widespread use of gasoline company credit cards. Stores classified as Other Services are least likely to offer credit and there is no difference between the blacks and whites of Harlem in this category. The chief difference between Harlem blacks and whites is to be found in the low-cost and high-cost categories, where whites are much more likely than blacks to extend credit. That black merchants have fewer resources to cope with credit or are less able to manage credit accounts becomes evident when we read across the rows of Table 3.8. For each type of business, white merchants in Harlem and Bay Ridge are more likely than the black merchants of Harlem to extend credit to customers.

Merchants who did extend credit were asked the proportion of their business consisting of credit sales. The greater proportion of whites in such businesses as furniture stores, which rely heavily on credit, is shown by the fact that more than one-third of the whites (35 percent) compared with little more than one-quarter of the blacks (28 percent) who do extend credit, report that credit makes up more than half their sales. For 19 percent of the white credit merchants, credit sales account for more than 70 percent of the total, compared with 8 percent of the black credit merchants. None of the Bay Ridge merchants had credit sales that amounted to as much as one-half their total sales. Thus in terms of volume of credit sales, Bay Ridge is far behind Harlem, although 57 percent of the Bay Ridge merchants, approximately the same proportion as that of the white Harlem merchants, extend credit.

Whether differences between Harlem black and white merchants regarding their use of credit reflects differences in types of businesses can be seen in Table 3.9. This table is

TABLE 3.7
EXTENSION OF CREDIT (in percentages)

Credit Policy	Harlem Merchants		Bay Ridge Merchants
	Blacks	Whites	
Currently offers credit	34	53	59
Used to, but no longer does	11	2	—
Has never offered credit	55	45	41
Total	100	100	100
n	(122)	(105)	(51)

TABLE 3.8
PERCENTAGE OFFERING CREDIT,
BY TYPE OF BUSINESS

Type of Business	Harlem Merchants				Bay Ridge Merchants	
	Blacks		Whites			
	%	n	%	n	%	n
Automotive services	77	(13)	87	(8)	89	(9)
Other services	26	(38)	28	(18)	[a]	(4)
Low-cost items	25	(44)	53	(40)	52	(23)
High-cost items	33	(24)	55	(36)	53	(15)

a. Base figure too small to yield reliable percentages.

TABLE 3.9
PERCENTAGE OF MERCHANTS FOR WHOM
CREDIT TRANSACTIONS ACCOUNT FOR AT LEAST HALF
OF SALES BY TYPE OF BUSINESS AMONG
MERCHANTS WHO EXTEND CREDIT

Type of Business	Harlem Merchants				Bay Ridge Merchants	
	Blacks		Whites			
	%	n	%	n	%	n
Automotive services	44	(9)	14	(7)	0	(7)
Other services	29	(7)	20	(5)	0	(2)
Small-cost items	17	(12)	17	(18)	0	(11)
High-cost items	25	(8)	67	(18)	0	(7)

limited to those who extend any form of credit and reports the percentage of such merchants whose business is made up of 50 percent or more of credit transactions.

The first thing to be noted in Table 3.9 is the minor role played by credit in the Bay Ridge community, for none of the relatively few merchants there who extends credit has credit transactions comprising 50 percent of his business. This is true regardless of type of business. But Table 3.9 shows marked differences between the Harlem blacks and whites. Perhaps the most striking finding is revealed by the base figures. Relatively few blacks, regardless of their type of business, extend credit. Although the small base figure must be approached with caution, it would seem that the blacks in automotive services and Other Services have more of a credit trade than the whites. In stores selling low-cost items there is no difference between the two groups of Harlem merchants; in stores selling high-cost items, credit transactions are far more important to the white businessman than to the black (67 percent compared with 25 percent have 50 percent or more of their sales accounted for by credit transactions). Since credit arrangements are most appropriate for high-cost items, the racial discrepancy again raises questions about the training of blacks in the world of consumer credit.

Black and white merchants in Harlem differ in both the extent and type of credit they offer. Almost all the credit extended by the blacks is *book* credit, the informal variety of credit typified by the corner grocer's entry in a ledger of the amount owed under the customer's name. Only 15 percent of the blacks extending credit deal in formal systems of credit, such as the installment contract, the credit card, or revolving credit. In contrast, almost half the white credit merchants (48 percent) extend the formal, contractual type of credit. Furthermore, none of the black businessmen require their credit customers to fill out a credit application, whereas twelve do of the white merchants who extend credit. To what extent is formal credit, as opposed to book credit, merely a factor of type of business? Table 3.10 shows the percentage of credit merchants offering formal credit in the three samples according to type of business.

The most striking finding in Table 3.10 is the vast discrepancy in the category of high-cost items between the blacks and the whites of Harlem and Bay Ridge. These are the types of stores that are most likely to extend formal credit. Not only are the black owners of such stores less likely to extend credit of any kind, but those who do are much less likely than their white counterparts to extend formal credit. Clearly there is a gap here between black and white businessmen in Harlem. The blacks appear much less receptive to formal credit, and to the extent that the community needs credit to buy expensive items, the white merchants seem to be more ready than the black merchants to meet this need.

The low-income merchant is generally believed to engage in more bargaining with customers than the general market retailer, that is, he is less likely to operate a "one-price" store. When the merchants were asked whether they maintain their prices or permit bargaining, the great majority of both black and white merchants claimed that they did maintain their prices. Nonetheless, whites were more likely than blacks to permit bargaining (20 percent versus 12 percent), but this rather small difference might be due entirely to the blacks being overrepresented in service-type businesses. Here, too, it is useful to compare the white merchants in Harlem with those in Bay Ridge. Only 11 percent of the Bay Ridge merchants engage in bargaining, a rate only one-half that of the white merchants in Harlem.

Whether the differences in bargaining reflect differences in type of business can be seen from Table 3.11. Again we must be cautious of the percentages based on small bases; e.g., the whites in automotive services both in Harlem and Bay Ridge, and the Bay Ridge merchants classified in Other Services. Bargaining does tend to increase as the cost of the item increases in all the samples. With the exception of automotive services, Harlem whites are more likely than blacks to engage in bargaining. The Bay Ridge merchants are least likely to permit haggling in stores selling expensive items. In view of the belief that haggling is widespread in ghetto furniture and appliance stores, it is somewhat odd that only a minority of the whites and blacks claim that they permit it. Perhaps this is one area where our merchants were more guarded. In any case, this selling technique is more prevalent among Harlem whites in three of the four types of stores. Only in automotive services, where the bases are small, do blacks seem more prone to bargaining.

Promotional Activities

Differences exist among black and white Harlem merchants with respect to three promotional activities: advertising, sales, and window displays. Black merchants are somewhat more likely than Harlem whites to invest in advertising, but they are not nearly so likely to have sales (partly, we suppose, because their types of business do not lend themselves readily to sales) or rely on window displays. Fifty-four percent of the blacks and 48 percent of the whites reported spending money on advertising. Differences are greater when we compare the type of advertising. The whites who advertise rely on window displays (22 percent versus 8 percent of the blacks) whereas blacks tend to use mass media—newspapers and radio—23 percent compared with 14 percent of the whites.

Only about 27 percent of the black merchants of Harlem in contrast with 58 percent of the Harlem white merchants, reported conducting sales.[3] White businessmen are not only more likely to have sales, but they conduct them more frequently. Thus 42 percent of the Harlem whites who have sales either have them continually or at least once a week, compared with only 17 percent of the blacks who have sales at all.

Interviewers were asked to check whether the business establishment used window displays. Only 54 percent of the black-owned businesses compared with 72 percent of the white-owned Harlem firms had window displays. Moreover, among those which did have window displays, white merchants were more likely to change them fairly often (at least monthly)—70 percent compared with 56 percent of the Harlem blacks. These findings on promotional activities are summarized in Table 3.12.

Bay Ridge merchants tend to engage in more promotional activities, although they are not quite as likely as the Harlem whites to conduct sales.

These three items dealing with promotion—advertising, sales, and window displays—are all positively correlated, permitting us to combine them in an index of promotional activity. Merchants who engage in at least two of these activities scored high on promotional activities. According to this index, 60 percent of the Harlem whites, 68 percent of the Bay Ridge merchants, but only 49 percent of the Harlem blacks score high. This discrepancy might be a consequence of the differences in size and type of business between black and white Harlem merchants.

Whether the difference in reliance upon promotional activities can be explained by size of establishment is shown in Table 3.13.

The columns show that promotional activities tend to increase with size of firm. At least the small firms in each sample are most likely to shun promotions. Oddly enough, those of medium size are most apt to score high on promotion. When size is held constant, the small black-owned firms are more likely to score high than the small white-owned Harlem firms, but in the medium and large categories, the Harlem whites are more likely to engage in promotional activities. On each size level, the Bay Ridge merchants are most likely to score high.

Advertising, sales, and window displays, the items that comprise our promotional activity index, are undoubtedly more appropriate for some businesses than for others. Thus when all three samples are combined, we find that 46 percent

TABLE 3.10

PERCENTAGE OF CREDIT MERCHANTS OFFERING
FORMAL CREDIT, BY TYPE OF BUSINESS

| Type of Business | Harlem Merchants | | | | Bay Ridge Merchants | |
| | Blacks | | Whites | | | |
	%	n	%	n	%	n
Automotive services	30	(10)	57	(7)	100	(8)
Other services	0	(10)	40	(5)	0	(2)
Low-cost items	9	(11)	19	(21)	25	(12)
High-cost items	25	(8)	85	(20)	87	(8)

TABLE 3.11

PERCENTAGE OF MERCHANTS WHO ENGAGE IN
BARGAINING, BY TYPE OF BUSINESS

| Type of Business | Harlem Merchants | | | | Bay Ridge Merchants | |
| | Blacks | | Whites | | | |
	%	n	%	n	%	n
Automotive services	15	(13)	0	(8)	17	(6)
Other services	3	(37)	11	(18)	25	(4)
Low-cost items	15	(46)	20	(40)	4	(23)
High-cost items	21	(24)	30	(37)	14	(14)

TABLE 3.12

PROMOTIONAL ACTIVITIES OF FIRM
WITHIN EACH SAMPLE

| | Harlem Merchants | | | | Bay Ridge Merchants | |
| | Blacks | | Whites | | | |
	%	n	%	n	%	n
Investing in advertising	54	(124)	48	(106)	77	(52)
Conducting sales	27	(112)	58	(103)	48	(52)
Window displays	54	(116)	72	(101)	100	(50)

of the automotive services and 34 percent of the Other Services score high on promotion, compared with 61 percent of the low-cost-item stores and 73 percent* of the high-cost-item stores. Table 3.14 shows these relationships separately within each of the three samples of businessmen.

The pattern for promotional activity is quite similar between Harlem blacks and whites but is quite different when these groups are compared with Bay Ridge merchants. Among blacks, there is a steady increase in promotional activity from automotive services to Other Services to low-cost items to high-cost items and (except for a reversal in the two service categories) the same is true for the Harlem whites. Among the Bay Ridge merchants, the nine merchants in automotive services are most likely to engage in promotional activities as all but one of the nine score high on the index, and the 25 merchants in low-cost merchandising are more likely to score high on promotional activity than those selling high-cost items. Comparing Harlem blacks and whites within the same type of store, we find no consistent differences. The few whites in automotive services rely somewhat more on promotion than do the blacks in this category. The blacks in the Other Services category score higher on promotional activity than the whites, whereas the reverse is true for stores selling high-cost items; there is no difference at all between the groups in the low-cost-item category. Thus, whether blacks or whites in Harlem rely on promotion is strongly influenced by type of business.

Interviewers' Ratings of Stores

Interviewers were asked to rate establishments on a number of characteristics such as cleanliness, layout of stock, lighting, interior painting, display of stock, and modernity of the store-front. On most of these ratings there was little difference between black- and white-owned establishments. White-owned stores scored higher on modernity of store-front, 40 percent receiving the highest rating compared with

31 percent of the black-owned stores. The largest difference occurred on the amount of stock displayed, with 60 percent of the white-owned stores rated high compared with 45 percent of the black-owned stores. (On this dimension, 75 percent of the Bay Ridge stores received the highest rating) White-owned stores in Harlem were more likely than black-owned stores to have air-conditioning (47 percent versus 36 percent). White-owned stores were also more likely to have a store-front gate (78 percent versus 64 percent). On such matters as cleanliness, lighting, and freshness of paint, black-owned stores were rated as high as the white-owned stores. White-owned stores were more likely to be rated as having dirty floors (15 percent compared with 8 percent).

As noted, the one rating that showed some difference between Harlem blacks and whites concerned the stock on display. This, however, turns out to depend, in part, on type of store (Table 3.15).

The figures for the two service categories can be discounted partly because the base figures are so small and partly because it is not clear what "well-stocked" means for these stores. Of more relevance are the patterns found for the stores selling low- and high-cost merchandise. In the low-cost category there is virtually no difference between Harlem whites and blacks as fewer than one-half in each group receive the "well-stocked" rating. Bay Ridge stores in this category do better than both Harlem blacks and whites. But in stores selling high-cost merchandise, those owned by Harlem whites receive a substantially higher rating than those owned by blacks. This finding may reflect differences in capitalization. To display a large amount of goods in a store selling high-cost merchandise undoubtedly requires substantial capital; hence black-owned stores in this category might well be at a competitive disadvantage. Data on this speculation will be presented in the next chapter where problems that merchants have raising capital are examined.

TABLE 3.13
PERCENTAGE SCORING HIGH ON PROMOTION INDEX, BY SIZE OF ESTABLISHMENT

| | Harlem Merchants | | | | Bay Ridge Merchants | |
| | Blacks | | Whites | | | |
Size of Establishment	%	n	%	n	%	n
Small	47	(77)	38	(29)	50	(26)
Medium	56	(30)	76	(34)	87	(15)
Large	50	(16)	61	(43)	84	(12)

TABLE 3.14
PERCENTAGE SCORING HIGH ON PROMOTION INDEX, BY TYPE OF ESTABLISHMENT

| | Harlem Merchants | | | | Bay Ridge Merchants | |
| | Blacks | | Whites | | | |
Type of Establishment	%	n	%	n	%	n
Automotive services	23	(13)	38	(8)	89	(9)
Other services	39	(41)	21	(19)	50	(4)
Low-cost items	58	(46)	59	(41)	68	(25)
High-cost items	63	(24)	84	(38)	60	(15)

TABLE 3.15
PERCENTAGE OF FIRMS RATED AS WELL-STOCKED, BY TYPE OF ESTABLISHMENT[a]

| | Harlem Merchants | | | | Bay Ridge Merchants | |
| | Blacks | | Whites | | | |
Type of Establishment	%	n	%	n	%	n
Automotive services	63	(8)	60	(5)	44	(9)
Other services	40	(25)	64	(11)	100	(4)
Low-cost items	43	(44)	45	(40)	83	(23)
High-cost items	48	(21)	74	(38)	77	(13)

a. The base figures shown in parentheses are smaller than in comparable tables because a number of stores were not rated on this dimension.

Record-Keeping Practices

One purpose of this study was to assess record-keeping practices of black and white businessmen in Harlem. Among the queries on this theme was one on whether the store-keeper had a cash register and if not, whether he used an adding machine. From Table 3.16 we see that Harlem whites were more likely than blacks to have these machines for keeping track of sales and for storing money. Surprisingly, blacks were not far behind Bay Ridge merchants.

More than one-fifth of the black owners had neither a cash register nor an adding machine, compared with only 7 percent of the Harlem white owners. But almost as many in the control group—19 percent—were also without either machine. Those who did have cash registers were asked whether their register had a tape; almost as many of the black owners answered in the affirmative as white owners (76 percent versus 81 percent). Those who did have tapes in their registers were then asked whether they checked their tapes daily. The blacks were not as likely to respond to this question (17 percent gave no reply versus 6 percent of the whites); among those who did answer, there was no differ-ence in the percentage who said they checked the tapes (about 90 percent in each group).

It would seem that whether a merchant has a cash register would be related to the size of his store. This expectation, however, is *not* borne out by the data, at least among Harlem merchants. As Table 3.17 shows, having a cash register is related to size of establishment only among the Bay Ridge merchants. Among Harlem merchants, both black and white, small stores are slightly *more* likely than large ones to have cash registers.

The merchants were also asked whether they kept sales slips. On this item of record-keeping, blacks do better than whites (61 percent versus 54 percent). Those who both kept sales slips and had cash registers with tapes (a minority in each group) were asked whether they checked sales slips against the tape. On this technique of record-keeping, the minority of whites with both systems do better than the minority of blacks; 79 percent of them compared with 63 percent of the blacks claimed that they checked sales slips against the tape.

The good businessman presumably keeps records that enable him to compare his sales during any period of the year with sales in the comparable period of the previous year. Again, Harlem whites are more likely than blacks to be able to make such comparisons (96 percent versus 87 percent). In both groups, the proportion who can make these comparisons is quite high. A follow-up question asked whether the businessman *usually* makes such period-to-period comparisons; again the whites are slightly ahead (93 percent versus 86 percent).

On the record-keeping activities considered so far, relatively little difference has been found between black and white Harlem merchants. Whites are more likely to have cash registers; blacks are more likely to keep sales slips. Whites are more likely than blacks (among those who could do this) to check sales slips against the cash register tape, and the great majority of both groups are able to compare one year's sales with the previous year.

Financial Statements and Inventory

It is the mark of the good businessman to keep systematic records of money taken in and money spent on the business. In this respect, there is no difference between black and white merchants; virtually all of them (96 percent of the blacks and 97 percent of the whites) claimed that they kept such records. Those who did keep these records were asked how often they had financial statements prepared. With respect to frequency, a striking difference is found between Harlem blacks and whites. The blacks are much more likely than the whites to have statements prepared a number of times a year. Thus 69 percent of the blacks but only 36 percent of the whites have financial statements prepared at least quarterly. (The Bay Ridge merchants fall between, as 52 percent have financial statements prepared that frequently.) More than half the Harlem whites (54 percent) but only one-quarter of the blacks (25 percent) prepare financial statements only once a year. Moreover, almost all the merchants in both groups (94 percent of the blacks and 98 percent of the whites) have these statements prepared for them by a professional, generally an accountant.

The sharp difference between Harlem blacks and whites regarding the frequency with which they have financial statements prepared raises several questions. Granted that having these statements is good business practice, does it follow that having them prepared *often* is a better business practice than having them prepared only once or twice a year? If frequent financial statements is a good business practice, why do white Harlem merchants, who have been in business longer and have larger establishments, lag behind the blacks? During the pre-test, some small Harlem black merchants explained to the researcher that they subscribed to an accounting service which prepared financial statements. The frequent financial statements may be more indicative of salesmanship in selling this service than of the business acumen of the merchant who subscribes to the service. Support for this view is provided when frequency is related to size of firm (Table 3.18).

In none of the three samples is there any consistent relationship between size of firm and frequency of financial statements. And yet the table is informative. The largest proportion of black-owned firms that have frequent statements prepared turn out to be the small ones (75 percent). Since the majority of black-owned businesses are small, the overall rate is quite high. The rate is lowest among black-owned medium-sized firms, although among whites, it is highest for firms of this size. The striking finding in Table 3.18 is the low rate of frequent financial statements of the

TABLE 3.16
USE OF CASH REGISTERS AND ADDING MACHINES
(in percentages)

| | Harlem Merchants | | Bay Ridge Merchants |
	Blacks	Whites	
Has cash register	69	81	77
Uses adding machine instead	9	12	4
Has neither	22	7	19
Total	100	100	100
n	(119)	(106)	(52)

TABLE 3.17
PERCENTAGE WITH A CASH REGISTER,
BY SIZE OF ESTABLISHMENT

| | Harlem Merchants | | | | Bay Ridge Merchants | |
| | Blacks | | Whites | | | |
Size of Establishment	%	n	%	n	%	n
Small	69	(73)	83	(29)	65	(26)
Medium	77	(30)	88	(34)	80	(15)
Large	67	(15)	74	(43)	92	(12)

TABLE 3.18
PERCENTAGE OF FIRMS HAVING FINANCIAL
STATEMENTS PREPARED FOUR OR MORE TIMES PER YEAR,
BY SIZE OF FIRM

| | Harlem Merchants | | | | Bay Ridge Merchants | |
| | Blacks | | Whites | | | |
Size of Establishment	%	n	%	n	%	n
Small	75	(73)	35	(26)	46	(24)
Medium	54	(28)	48	(31)	42	(12)
Large	69	(16)	28	(40)	75	(12)

large white-owned firms in Harlem. The modal category of white-owned stores in Harlem are those of large size and it is in precisely this category that the smallest proportion of establishments (only 28 percent) have financial statements prepared at least quarterly. In this respect, the large white-owned stores in Harlem are not only very different from the black-owned stores of the same size but also from the large stores in the Bay Ridge control group. Thus Table 3.18 poses two difficult questions. First, why are the black owners of small stores especially likely to have frequent financial statements, much more so than the white owners of small stores both in Harlem and Bay Ridge? And second, why are the white owners of large Harlem stores, the men with presumably the most business experience, least likely to have financial statements prepared frequently? The situation of the black owners of small stores might well reflect their subscribing to an accounting service, and the frequency of their statements might indicate the salesmanship of the purveyors of this service, independent of its value. But why the white owners of large stores rely less on financial statements than not only their black counterparts but their counterparts in Bay Ridge as well remains a mystery.

Businessmen were also asked about the value of these statements for their business. Some businessmen have financial statements prepared for tax purposes only and make little use of them as a guide to operating their business; others rely heavily on statements as an aid to business decisions. Thus when asked what they learned from financial statements, 15 percent of the Harlem blacks and whites admitted that they learned practically nothing, and had them prepared for tax purposes only; 85 percent in each group reported that these statements permitted them to assess the profit of their business. In Bay Ridge, the same proportion of businessmen found financial statements of value, 84 percent. Although the same proportions of Harlem blacks and whites found financial statements useful to their business, a further question revealed differences. All the businessmen were asked whether financial statements were of great, fair, or little importance in operating their business. On this subjective rating, black businessmen ascribed more importance to financial statements, 68 percent of them compared with 57 percent of the Harlem whites considering them very important. In the Bay Ridge sample, 66 percent reported that financial statements were very important. Although the frequency of financial statements was not related to size of firm, the importance of such statements shows some relationship to size. With one slight reversal among the Bay Ridge merchants, this pattern holds within each sample (Table 3.19).

The association between size of firm and importance of financial statement is most evident among the blacks; but even among Harlem whites and the Bay Ridge merchants, those owning large establishments consider these statements more important than those owning smaller ones. This is so even though the blacks who own small stores have such statements prepared more frequently. In short, there is a disjunction between the frequency of these statements and the importance attributed to them. Of some significance is the fact that on each level of firm size, the blacks assign more importance to financial statements than do the Harlem whites. On this measure of "good business practice," the Harlem blacks thus do better. Not only do they have financial statements prepared more often—which may or may not be a good thing—but they pay more attention to the financial statement which most judges would agree *is* a good thing.

Another aspect of records concerns inventory-taking which serves such functions as alerting the businessman to the need of reordering or the need to hold sales in order to reduce slow-moving merchandise. Thirteen black businessmen and four Harlem whites did not reply to our question of whether they had a system of keeping track of stock. Of those who did answer, slightly more blacks than Harlem whites answered affirmatively, 74 percent versus 70 percent. (In this respect, both groups of Harlem businessmen do better than the control group in Bay Ridge, where only 63 percent had a system for inventory.) Those who said they had a system of keeping track of stock were asked whether they kept a perpetual inventory. Seventy-four percent of the blacks, 64 percent of the Harlem whites, and 69 percent of the Bay Ridge merchants answered affirmatively. Those who did not have a system were asked whether they occasionally took physical inventory (that is, go through the store and count the items on the shelves). Here we find that Harlem whites are more likely than blacks to take physical inventory (76 percent compared with 62 percent, and the comparable figure for the Bay Ridge sample is 67 percent). When the various questions about keeping track of stock are pooled, we find the results that appear in Table 3.20.

When the data on inventory are assessed, we find that blacks are less likely than Harlem whites to take inventory, with the Bay Ridge merchants falling between. The difference between Harlem blacks and whites on this matter of taking inventory is not a result of the difference in size of establishment even though the larger stores are more likely to have some system for taking inventory. This can be seen from Table 3.21.

There is little difference between the black and white merchants in the small-size category with respect to inventory, but as size of store increases, so does the gap between blacks and whites. In the medium-size category, we find a difference of 8 percentage points in favor of the Harlem whites; in the large category, this increases to a difference of 27 percentage points. On this aspect of record-keeping, the whites in Harlem excel their black counterparts because the blacks who own large stores pay less attention to inventory than do whites who own large stores.

When type of firm is taken into account (Table 3.22), the pattern is rather irregular. No differences are found among the three groups of merchants in automotive services and

TABLE 3.19
PERCENTAGE CONSIDERING FINANCIAL STATEMENTS
VERY IMPORTANT, BY SIZE OF ESTABLISHMENT

| | Harlem Merchants | | | | Bay Ridge Merchants | |
| | Blacks | | Whites | | | |
Size of Establishment	%	n	%	n	%	n
Small	64	(72)	52	(27)	63	(24)
Medium	74	(27)	52	(33)	55	(11)
Large	81	(16)	64	(39)	83	(12)

TABLE 3.20
INVENTORY PRACTICES (in percentages)

| | Harlem Merchants | | Bay Ridge Merchants |
Inventory Practice	Blacks	Whites	
Perpetual inventory	50	44	43
Physical inventory	24	40	35
No inventory	26	16	22
Total	100	100	100
n	(123)	(105)	(51)

TABLE 3.21
PERCENTAGE TAKING INVENTORY,
BY SIZE OF ESTABLISHMENT

| | Harlem Merchants | | | | Bay Ridge Merchants | |
| | Blacks | | Whites | | | |
Size of Establishment	%	n	%	n	%	n
Small	76	(75)	79	(28)	72	(25)
Medium	77	(30)	85	(34)	80	(15)
Large	59	(17)	86	(43)	91	(11)

only slight differences occur among the Low-Cost Item merchants. Blacks do as well as Harlem whites and better than the Bay Ridge merchants in the High-Cost category; only in Other Services do the blacks lag behind the two groups of whites. The greater likelihood of Harlem whites than of Harlem blacks having a system for keeping track of stock thus turns out to be due entirely to the whites in the Other Services category.

Having reviewed a number of aspects of record-keeping, from having cash registers and keeping sales slips to having financial statements prepared and taking inventory, the safest conclusion, perhaps, is that there is little difference between Harlem blacks and whites. Although the blacks tend to have smaller businesses than the whites, they seem to be as conscientious, if not more so, in keeping business records.

Just as the various components of promotional activities were interrelated, so, too, are these various aspects of record-keeping. Thus, the businessman with a cash register is also more likely to keep sales slips, compare sales slips with the tape, make comparisions between this year's and last year's sales, and have some system of keeping track of stock. We have thus combined these items into one general index of record-keeping activities. That the black businessmen of Harlem do as well if not better than their white counterparts in the area of record-keeping is suggested by this index. Some 55 percent of the Harlem blacks, 53 percent of the Harlem whites, and 47 percent of the Bay Ridge merchants score high on this index. We find that a good score on record-keeping increases with size of establishment in each sample (see Table 3.23), but perhaps more importantly, the Harlem blacks generally score better than the Harlem whites in each size group.

The merchants least likely to have good record-keeping systems are the small merchants in the Bay Ridge control group, but the medium and large firms in that sample do better in this respect than the Harlem merchants of comparable size. Among the small- and medium-sized firms, the

TABLE 3.22
PERCENTAGE TAKING INVENTORY,
BY TYPE OF ESTABLISHMENT [a]

| | Harlem Merchants | | | | Bay Ridge Merchants | |
| | Blacks | | Whites | | | |
Type of Business	%	n	%	n	%	n
Automotive services	75	(12)	75	(7)	75	(7)
Other services	50	(31)	78	(19)	100	(4)
Low-cost items	85	(45)	81	(40)	76	(25)
High-cost items	92	(24)	92	(36)	79	(15)

a. Again the base figures are reduced because a number of merchants did not answer this question.

TABLE 3.23
PERCENTAGE OF FIRMS WITH RELATIVELY HIGH
SCORE ON RECORD-KEEPING ACTIVITIES,
BY SIZE OF FIRM

| | Harlem Merchants | | | | Bay Ridge Merchants | |
| | Blacks | | Whites | | | |
Size of Establishment	%	n	%	n	%	n
Small	53	(76)	41	(29)	27	(26)
Medium	57	(30)	50	(34)	67	(15)
Large	63	(16)	63	(43)	67	(12)

blacks are more likely to score high on record keeping than the whites, and only among the large firms do the whites of Harlem come off as well as the blacks.

Table 3.24 compares the merchants in the three samples on record-keeping within each type of business. The results for automotive services should perhaps be ignored since the base figures are so small, but the patterns in the other three groups of businesses are interesting. The blacks score much better than the Harlem whites on record-keeping in the Other Services category and in stores selling low-cost items. But in the stores selling high-cost items, the whites of Harlem far exceed the blacks on record-keeping. This is particularly surprising because we have already seen that large, high-cost white-owned stores are not as likely to have financial statements prepared frequently, one of the items comprising the record-keeping index. We have already noted some of the relative disadvantages of the black-owned stores selling high-cost merchandise and the next chapter will document some more. Table 3.24 makes it clear that the blacks in this category are not as adept as the whites in keeping business records. In the Bay Ridge control group, the results are rather confusing. Merchants selling low-cost items keep better records than those selling high-cost items (as is true of the Harlem blacks) but record-keeping scores in other types of businesses bear no relationship to those of Harlem merchants.

Having considered the relevance of size of establishment and type of store for record-keeping, we turn now to a consideration of the impact of business training on record-keeping. The connection between the index of business background developed in the previous chapter and record-keeping can be seen from Table 3.25.

The business background of the black merchants has virtually no impact on their tendency to keep records. If anything, among the blacks these characteristics tend to be negatively related, as proportionately more of those with a *weak* background in business score *high* on record-keeping.

TABLE 3.24

PERCENTAGE SCORING RELATIVELY HIGH ON RECORD-KEEPING INDEX, BY TYPE OF BUSINESS

| Type of Business | Harlem Merchants | | | | Bay Ridge Merchants | |
| | Blacks | | Whites | | | |
	%	n	%	n	%	n
Automotive services	23	(13)	50	(8)	44	(9)
Other services	63	(40)	53	(19)	25	(4)
Low-cost items	63	(46)	37	(41)	56	(25)
High-cost items	42	(24)	71	(38)	40	(15)

TABLE 3.25

PERCENTAGE SCORING RELATIVELY HIGH ON RECORD-KEEPING, BY SCORE IN BUSINESS BACKGROUND INDEX

| Business Background | Harlem Merchants | | | | Bay Ridge Merchants | |
| | Blacks | | Whites | | | |
	%	n	%	n	%	n
Weak	58	(58)	27	(25)	50	(6)
Moderate	49	(41)	58	(55)	32	(28)
Strong	50	(22)	68	(25)	68	(19)

But among Harlem whites there is a strong positive relationship: the more knowledgeable they are about the business world, the more likely they are to maintain an adequate record-keeping system. The ones who have not been previously exposed to a business culture tend to be lax in their practices, much more so than the comparable group of blacks. Whites with only a moderate business background show a marked improvement in record-keeping, as their chances of scoring high exceed those with a weak background by 31 percentage points. And the probability of whites scoring high increases still further among those with a strong business background. Whereas the blacks with little exposure to a business culture do much better than the whites in this group, the reverse is true among those with moderate or strong exposures to business. There are too few Bay Ridge merchants with a weak business background to give credence to the percentage for this group, but from the percentages for those in the moderate and strong categories, it would seem that the positive relationship holds in this sample as well. Thus, the Bay Ridgers with a strong exposure to business are much more likely to keep good records than are those in the middle category.

Summary

We have examined a number of aspects of the manner in which the businessmen in the three samples conduct their business. The analysis began by examining the racial composition of their work force, and the findings showed that the black merchants in Harlem were somewhat more likely than the Harlem whites to employ blacks, but this did not indicate any preference of the whites for employees of their own kind, for they were more likely than the blacks to employ Spanish-speaking persons. This difference is largely explained by the location of the store within Harlem and type of business. Little difference between black and white Harlem merchants was found in respect to the racial composition of their customers.

Black-owned establishments were much more likely to remain open more hours and days per week, even when size and type of business were held constant. When credit policies were examined, Harlem whites were found to be more likely than blacks to extend credit, particularly the more formal type of credit represented by the installment credit contract and credit cards. This difference was partially explained by the whites being more heavily represented in stores selling high-cost merchandise; but even when type of store was held constant, the whites of Harlem were more likely to extend credit. This finding called attention to one respect in which black-owned businesses may place strain on the needs of a low-income black community. To the extent that credit is needed in such a community, it may well be that white merchants are more responsive than black merchants to this need.

With respect to promotional activities, blacks were found to be somewhat more likely than whites to advertise through the mass media but were not as likely to conduct sales or use window displays. An index comprised of these three promotional activities showed the Harlem whites scoring higher than the blacks although not so high as the merchants in the Bay Ridge control group. When size of firm was taken into account, the small black-owned firms relied more on promotion than the small white-owned firms, but in the medium and large categories, the whites scored higher on promotion than the blacks.

The white-owned stores received a higher rating than the black-owned stores on the amount of merchandise on display, a difference that was partially a function of type of business. But the white-owned stores selling high-cost merchandise were judged to be better stocked than the comparable stores owned by blacks. This, in turn, suggested that the whites in this category had more capital at their disposal than the blacks.

There was little difference between Harlem blacks and whites on a number of aspects of record-keeping, such as having cash registers, keeping sales slips, using financial statements, and taking inventory. In fact, as the record-keeping index showed, the blacks do somewhat better than the whites on this dimension of business practices. The one marked difference found was that the blacks were much more likely to have financial statements prepared frequently, a function of the small black-owned stores doing so, and the large white-owned stores not doing so.

Upon comparing the black and white businessmen on their business practices, perhaps the safest conclusion is that there are few major differences. The blacks and whites seem equally well attuned to sound business practices, and if the black firms are smaller and confronted with more problems (an issue we shall examine in the next chapter), the blame clearly cannot be placed on their ignorance or naiveté about sound business practices.

Chapter 4

PROBLEMS OF HARLEM MERCHANTS

The primary concern of this study is to shed light on the problems of black and white merchants of Harlem. The areas that were explored include finding competent help, establishing credit with suppliers and banks, obtaining insurance, and coping with security hazards. Each of these threats to the stability of an enterprise is discussed in this chapter.

Personnel Problems

It might seem incongruous that the merchants of Harlem would have trouble finding competent help. The mass media periodically report the high unemployment rate in this ghetto area, and they depict Harlem as a community that would welcome opportunities for gainful employment. But this is only a partial picture of reality. It must be remembered that Harlem residents have a low educational level and a limited range of acquired skills. Given these restrictions, it might well be that the Harlem merchant would not be able to fill all his job vacancies with qualified people from the local labor market. Another constraint that must be borne in mind is the narrow profit margin of the small merchant. If he is forced to recruit outside the neighborhood, he may not be able to bid enough for skilled manpower. Furthermore, he may find that he has to pay more to attract workers willing to work in a low-income community.

The merchants in the three samples were asked if they had a problem finding competent help. Forty-three percent of the Harlem merchants reported that this was indeed a problem; and surprisingly, the black businessmen were more likely to answer affirmatively than the whites (47 percent versus 38 percent). Finding competent help turns out to be as much a problem for retailers in a white, middle-class community, for among the Bay Ridge merchants the frequency is the same as it is for the blacks of Harlem (47 percent), greater than for the Harlem whites.

Perhaps one reason the blacks experience difficulty more frequently than the whites is that their firms are smaller. Small stores are not likely to be able to afford to pay premium wages. But the data indicate that this is not the case. Finding competent help turns out to be a more severe problem for the large stores, as the percentages in Table 4.1 demonstrate.

In all three samples, small store owners are *least* likely to have trouble finding qualified personnel. This may simply mean that the small store owner has little *need* for help in addition to himself and his immediate family members. The disparity between the blacks and whites of Harlem is due mainly to the small stores. For some reason the blacks who own small stores are much more likely than the whites owning small stores to report this problem.

The merchants who did have a problem finding competent help were asked to explain why. Even though not all of them offered a reason, it is of some interest to compare the Harlem whites with the blacks, and then to compare each of these groups with the control sample. The reasons are presented in Table 4.2.

The explanations offered by the black and white Harlem businessmen are quite similar. In both groups, the chief complaint is that prospective employees lack training and experience—a finding in keeping with the nature of a ghetto community. The next reason most frequently mentioned by both the blacks and whites of Harlem is the unreliability of employees. The largest difference between these two groups is found in the last row of Table 4.2. White merchants are more likely to say that prospective employees do not want to work in Harlem, indicating that they, more than the blacks, look for employees outside of Harlem. This interpretation is corroborated by the earlier finding that white businessmen are more likely than their black counterparts to employ whites. But the striking feature of the table remains the similarity of the reasons offered by both Harlem groups.

As can be seen from the third column of Table 4.2, the merchants in Bay Ridge give quite different reasons for personnel problems. Few of these merchants complain about unreliability of employees, and only a few attribute the problem to lack of training—the two reasons most common among the Harlem merchants. Their major difficulty stems from the fact that the persons in *their* particular labor market are not interested in retail work (almost half of them give this reason). The Bay Ridge merchants are also more likely than the Harlem merchants to mention their inability to meet wage demands. The marked differences between the Harlem and Bay Ridge merchants on this issue stem from their very different labor pools. Both the black and white businessmen of Harlem are apt to offer employment to local residents. In this low-income community, clerical and sales jobs provide attractive opportunities for economic improvement. In contrast, Bay Ridge merchants deal with a labor pool of young, educated whites for whom jobs in retail establishments have long since lost their appeal. The patterns in Table 4.2 point up the differential job opportunities of blacks and whites in

America today. The Harlem businessmen complain about the lack of skill in the black labor pool from which they hire their help. On the other hand, the white businessmen in a middle-class area find that they cannot compete with the extensive opportunities open to those in the white labor pool.

Problems With Suppliers

The small businessman in a ghetto area, especially the newly established owner, does not have assets that are attractive to suppliers. He has not had an opportunity to build up a credit rating, nor does he purchase stock in substantial quantities. Hence he cannot deal with the suppliers who provide goods for the lowest cost. As we have already seen, the black merchant in Harlem is more likely to have been in business for a relatively short time and his business tends to be smaller than that of the white owner. These two factors alone could place the black merchant at a competitive disadvantage vis-á-vis his white counterpart in commodity and financial exchange centers.

Retailers can obtain merchandise from three sources: the manufacturer, the wholesaler, or the jobber. These sources represent different economies to the retailer, and whether he deals with one or another is dependent upon the size of his orders. Those who can buy bulk deal directly with manu-facturers. (The manufacturer's shipping unit is ordinarily the carload.) Those who cannot buy in such substantial quanti-ties turn to the wholesaler who is the middle-man distributing case lots. Finally, those who can buy only in broken lots must deal with the jobber, a *second* middle-man, who buys his wares from the wholesaler. It is widely believed that the chief obstacle confronting the black businessman is his inability to make purchases large enough to permit circum-venting the jobber, to whom he pays extra handling charges. The data support this belief, although the picture is more complex than this exposition would suggest.

TABLE 4.1

**PERCENTAGE OF MERCHANTS WHO REPORT HAVING A
PROBLEM FINDING COMPETENT HELP, BY SIZE OF FIRM**

Size of Establishment	Harlem Merchants				Bay Ridge Merchants	
	Blacks		Whites			
	%	n	%	n	%	n
Small	44	(77)	14	(28)	27	(26)
Medium	52	(29)	49	(33)	67	(15)
Large	53	(17)	47	(43)	67	(12)

TABLE 4.2

MOST IMPORTANT REASON FOR PERSONNEL PROBLEMS
(in percentages)

Reasons for Personnel Problems	Harlem Merchants		Bay Ridge Merchants
	Blacks	Whites	
Poor training and experience	47	41	27
Unreliability (absenteeism; dishonesty; drinking)	25	28	5
Dislike for kind of establishment	10	6	46
Low interest in working of potential help	8	6	5
Demand for high wages	4	3	18
Dislike for Harlem location	6	16	—
Total	100	100	101
n	(49)	(32)	(22)

TABLE 4.3

**PERCENTAGE OF MERCHANTS REPORTING PROBLEMS
WITH SUPPLIERS, BY SIZE OF ESTABLISHMENT**

Size of Establishment	Harlem Merchants				Bay Ridge Merchants	
	Blacks		Whites			
	%	n	%	n	%	n
Small	17	(76)	24	(29)	8	(26)
Medium	17	(30)	21	(34)	27	(15)
Large	13	(15)	30	(43)	17	(12)

Were we limited to data on the perception of problems with suppliers, we would come to the startling conclusion that the white businessmen in Harlem, in spite of their greater tenure and size, have *more* problems than the blacks. When asked directly whether they have problems with suppliers, 16 percent of the blacks versus 26 percent of the Harlem whites answered affirmatively. In Bay Ridge, only 15 percent of the merchants said they had problems with suppliers.

As can be seen from Table 4.3, the Harlem blacks on each level of size of firm are less likely than Harlem whites to admit to problems with suppliers. Not only do proportionately fewer blacks perceive problems with suppliers whatever the size of the store, but size of store has no relationship to this response in any of the three samples. Among blacks, the owners of large establishments are least likely to report problems; among the whites, it is those in medium-sized stores; and among the Bay Ridge merchants, it is the small shopkeepers who are least likely to report this problem.

But *perception* of a problem with suppliers is not necessarily a true indication of the reality of the situation. It would seem that many businessmen, particularly black businessmen, interpreted this question to mean whether they had problems obtaining merchandise at all, not whether they had difficulty obtaining credit from suppliers or purchasing merchandise at advantageous prices. This conclusion stems from the data on the sources and financing of supplies.

The merchants were asked whether they bought from manufacturers, wholesalers, jobbers, or any combination of the three. Table 4.4 shows these data for the three samples of merchants.

It should be noted that the white merchants, whether from Harlem or Bay Ridge, are more likely than blacks to list multiple sources. As the first row of the table shows, the white merchants exercise their option of buying from manufacturers more often than the blacks. More than half the white merchants but only one-fifth of the black merchants buy at least some supplies from manufacturers. Table 4.4 shows that blacks do not deal any more frequently with the costliest supplier, the jobber. But these data do not report the degree of dependency on each type of supplier. This can be seen from Table 4.5 which combines those who buy from both wholesalers and manufacturers with those who buy exclusively from manufacturers.

When we consider those who deal primarily with only one source, we find further evidence of the competitive disadvantage of the black merchant. Twenty-eight percent of the whites in Harlem buy their entire stock mainly from manufacturers compared with 11 percent of the blacks. In the jobber class, the ratio of the percentages is reversed—23 percent of the blacks deal *only* with jobbers compared with 11 percent of the whites. In short, twice as many white merchants in Harlem deal exclusively with the most economical source of supply while twice as many blacks purchase all of their supplies from the costliest source. Can the tendency of the whites to deal with the most economical suppliers be explained by the large size of their firms? Table 4.6 shows that whites are more likely to deal with manufacturers, whatever the size of the establishment.

By reading down the columns, it can be seen that although the perception of a problem with suppliers is unrelated to size of firm, dealing with the most advantageous supplier—the manufacturer (either alone or in combination with the wholesaler)—clearly relates to size in each of the three groups. Controlling for size does little to alter the previously noted competitive disadvantage of the black merchants. Only in the large establishments do the blacks come close to the whites in the likelihood of buying from manufacturers and avoiding jobbers.

It would seem that type of supplier should also be related to type of store. But the data on this issue present a confusing picture. When the three samples are viewed as a whole in relating type of store to source of supplies, we find that the stores selling high-cost items are most likely to deal

TABLE 4.4
SOURCES OF SUPPLIES (in percentages)

Suppliers	Harlem Merchants		Bay Ridge Merchants
	Blacks	Whites	
Manufacturer	20	57	54
Wholesaler	69	64	77
Jobber	46	50	45
Total	135[a]	171[a]	176[a]
n	(117)	(104)	(53)

a. Percentages exceed 100 because of multiple sources.

TABLE 4.5
SOURCES OF SUPPLIES IN THE THREE SAMPLES
(in percentages)

Type of Supplier	Harlem Merchants		Bay Ridge Merchants
	Blacks	Whites	
Manufacturer only; manu- facturer and wholesaler	11	28	24
Wholesaler only	43	23	30
Jobber and others	23	38	36
Jobber only	23	11	9
Total	100	100	99

TABLE 4.6
PERCENTAGE OF MERCHANTS DEALING WITH MANUFACTURERS ONLY OR MANUFACTURERS AND WHOLESALERS, BY SIZE OF ESTABLISHMENT

Size of Establishment	Harlem Merchants				Bay Ridge Merchants	
	Blacks		Whites			
	%	n	%	n	%	n
Small	9	(71)	21	(28)	19	(26)
Medium	10	(30)	27	(33)	20	(15)
Large	27	(15)	33	(43)	42	(12)

with manufacturers either exclusively or in combination with wholesalers (41 percent), and stores selling low-cost items are least likely to buy from this class of distributors (11 percent); Other Services follows with 13 percent and the automotive services falls between the high and low points with 23 percent. The stores that are least likely to deal with manufacturers are the ones most likely to deal with the next most economical source, the wholesaler. Thus half the stores classified as Other Services buy only from wholesalers, as do 40 percent of the stores selling low-cost items, in contrast with only 15 percent of the high-cost-item stores and one-third of the automotive service stores. Establishments classified as Other Services show the highest rate—25 percent—of dealing exclusively with jobbers. Automotive services is not far behind with a rate of 20 percent. Only 12 percent of the stores selling high-cost items buy from jobbers, and the lowest rate for such costly buying practices is found among stores selling low-cost items (9 percent); yet it was this type of store that was least likely to deal with the most economical supplier, the manufacturer. In short, there do not seem to be any consistent patterns relating type of store to source of supplies.

Differences in the relationships of black and white businessmen with suppliers are also revealed by the mode of payment for merchandise. Retailers who have no credit with suppliers are required to pay cash on delivery (C.O.D.). Others can defer payment for 10, 30, or 60 days. Merchants with a high credit rating are offered the option of discounting their bills if payment is made within 10 days. The merchant can, of course, have different arrangements with different suppliers. When asked about paying his accounts, the merchant could answer the question in more than one way. As can be seen from Table 4.7, the black merchants in Harlem are more likely than the whites to have to pay cash-on-delivery, an indication that the suppliers regard the blacks as poor credit risks.

Fully two-thirds of the black businessmen are required to

pay C.O.D. for at least some of their supplies, compared with 31 percent of the white merchants in Harlem and only 17 percent of the Bay Ridge merchants. The difference is larger than the figures suggest for when we consider those who must pay C.O.D. for *all* their supplies, we find that this is true for 53 percent of the blacks compared with only 9 percent of the whites in Harlem and 11 percent of the Bay Ridge merchants. The blacks are not only more likely to pay C.O.D., but they are least able to take advantage of the most economical arrangement "2/10, net 30." This method is used by 29 percent of the Harlem whites and 40 percent of the Bay Ridge whites. The greater credit that white merchants have with their suppliers is indicated by the much larger percentage in both white groups that are given 30 days in which to make payment.[4]

Table 4.7 clearly shows that black merchants have more difficulty than the whites in getting credit from suppliers. In fact, they seem to have a problem greater than they themselves realize. We have noted that black merchants are less likely than the whites to report problems with suppliers. When asked whether they have trouble getting credit from suppliers, the black merchants were more ready than whites to concede this problem. Fifteen percent of the blacks admit to having difficulty in getting credit from suppliers compared with 8 percent of the Harlem whites and 2 percent of the Bay Ridge respondents. However, these subjective differences are not so marked as the objective differences shown in Table 4.7. The problem is greater than the black merchants perceive.

The tendency of the black merchants to pay C.O.D. for their merchandise is explained partly by the smaller size of their establishments, for when all samples are combined and size alone is related to method of payment, we find that 42 percent of the small stores pay C.O.D. for all their merchandise, compared with 21 percent of the medium-sized stores and only 12 percent of the large stores. However, size alone does not completely explain the difference. When size is held constant, black merchants still have the highest incidence of paying for all goods on delivery (Table 4.8).

The relationship between size and paying C.O.D. is accounted for by the black-owned establishments. Among Harlem whites, the pattern is irregular; and among the Bay Ridge merchants, the size pattern is inexplicably reversed. On each level of size, the largest percentage of merchants paying C.O.D. for supplies are the blacks. This finding confirms earlier results. Blacks are likely to have more disadvantageous arrangements for settling accounts with suppliers whatever the size of their establishments.

Type of business, too, does not explain the black-white differential in mode of paying for supplies. In the aggregate, the Other Services are most likely to pay C.O.D. for all of their supplies (38 percent); the stores selling high-cost items are least likely to pay this way (19 percent); and the automotive services and low-cost-item categories fall between these points (with 31 percent and 29 percent respectively). When type of business is held constant, black merchants are still more likely to pay C.O.D., as can be seen from the rows of Table 4.9.

The differences between the blacks and the whites—and also the Bay Ridge merchants—are pronounced for every type of establishment. This is especially true for the high-cost-item stores. The percentages for the blacks vary from 42 to 57 percent in contrast to the Harlem whites, which vary from 0 to 15 percent. We have already seen that the blacks selling high-cost merchandise deal most frequently with the highest-priced distributors, the jobbers, and now we find that more than half these merchants have no credit with their suppliers, a factor which both limits the amount of goods they can buy and places strains on their capital reserves.

The idea of cooperatives is being considered by the Harlem Commonwealth Council to enable black merchants to buy more economically. (Such cooperatives have been set up successfully in New York by Puerto Rican owners of Bodegas.) The merchants were asked two questions about

TABLE 4.7
MODE OF PAYMENT TO SUPPLIERS (in percentages)

| Mode of Payment | Harlem Merchants | | Bay Ridge Merchants |
	Blacks	Whites	
2% discount within 10 days	14	29	40
Within 30 days	31	63	44
Within 60 days	14	10	8
Cash-on-delivery	67	31	17
Total	126[a]	133[a]	109[a]
n	(121)	(104)	(53)

a. Percentages exceed 100% because of multiple modes of payment.

TABLE 4.8
PERCENTAGE OF MERCHANTS PAYING C.O.D. FOR ALL MERCHANDISE, BY SIZE OF ESTABLISHMENT

| Size of Establishment | Harlem Merchants | | | | Bay Ridge Merchants | |
| | Blacks | | Whites | | | |
	%	n	%	n	%	n
Small	66	(76)	10	(29)	8	(26)
Medium	35	(29)	12	(33)	13	(15)
Large	27	(15)	5	(42)	17	(12)

TABLE 4.9
PERCENTAGE OF MERCHANTS PAYING C.O.D. FOR MERCHANDISE, BY TYPE OF ESTABLISHMENT

| Type of Establishment | Harlem Merchants | | | | Bay Ridge Merchants | |
| | Blacks | | Whites | | | |
	%	n	%	n	%	n
Automotive services	42	(12)	13	(8)	33	(9)
Other services	51	(41)	11	(19)	25	(4)
Low-cost items	57	(44)	15	(41)	4	(25)
High-cost items	54	(24)	0	(36)	7	(15)

such cooperatives, the first being whether they thought a buying cooperative was a good idea. This question was designed to elicit not only their opinion of such an arrangement but also their familiarity with buying cooperatives. Thirteen percent of the black businessmen, 11 percent of the Harlem whites, and 11 percent of the Bay Ridge merchants did not understand the question or were unfamiliar with buying cooperatives. In addition, about 3 percent in each group offered no opinion. Of the Harlem merchants who did have an opinion, it is significant that 72 percent of the blacks had a positive attitude toward the idea, whereas only 46 percent of the whites did. Oddly enough, the Bay Ridge merchants were as receptive as the blacks to such a plan, as 74 percent of those with an opinion approved of buying cooperatives. The second question was more explicit. Regardless of how the first was answered, everyone was asked:

"Would you personally be interested in purchasing your merchandise or supplies by pooling orders with other merchants?"

Again, there is a marked difference between the black and white merchants of Harlem. Fifty-eight percent of the blacks said they would be interested in such a program compared with only 25 percent of the whites. The Bay Ridge merchants again proved more receptive than the Harlem whites with 55 percent expressing an interest in joint purchasing.[5] Since a majority of the blacks are willing to join buying co-ops, it would seem that they are more aware of their competitive disadvantage in dealings with suppliers than suggested by their responses to questions about problems with suppliers and obtaining credit from them. That the Harlem whites show much less interest in cooperatives than the Bay Ridge merchants might mean that they are reluctant to enter cooperatives with blacks, or it might mean simply that they do not feel any need to improve their competitive position in this manner.

The greater receptiveness of black merchants to buying

cooperatives is not a function of the smallness of their firms, for on each size level the blacks were more likely than the Harlem whites to respond affirmatively as can be seen from Table 4.10.

It should be noted that the black owners of large stores are even more receptive to cooperative buying than the owners of small stores. However the black merchants in Harlem choose to define their situation, the findings presented in this section indicate that they do have more problems with suppliers than do their white competitors and would presumably benefit more from buying cooperatives.

Problems in Raising Capital

A major asset of any businessman is a high credit rating—his capacity to raise capital by borrowing funds to meet payrolls, pay suppliers, renovate, or expand. We have already seen that the black businessman in Harlem is most likely to have problems with suppliers. An analogous pattern emerges when he attempts to raise capital. Merchants were asked whether raising capital for their business is a major problem. Some 39 percent of the black businessmen said that this was a major problem, compared with 21 percent of the Harlem whites and only 12 percent of those in Bay Ridge.

Apart from the difficulties they may have encountered, all merchants were asked whether, in fact, they had ever borrowed money for business purposes. Again we find a noticeable difference between the black and white businessmen of Harlem. Sixty-nine percent of the whites had borrowed money compared with 50 percent of the blacks. In the Bay Ridge control group, 56 percent (slightly more than the Harlem blacks) had borrowed for business purposes. That the whites in Harlem are more likely than the blacks to have borrowed money might simply reflect their greater need for loans rather than their greater ability to obtain them. To check this possibility, we asked those who had never borrowed for business purposes why they had not. The advantageous position of the white businessman is revealed by responses to this probe. Among Harlem whites who had never borrowed, 90 percent said they had never needed a loan and only 10 percent said they could not get one. Among blacks, 65 percent reported no need, and 35 percent said they could not get a loan. Among Bay Ridge merchants, the refusal rate was only five percent.

Whether these merchants actually have obtained business loans is positively correlated with the size of the establishment. The larger the establishment, the greater the likelihood that the owner has borrowed money for business purposes. Forty-six percent of the small establishments, 60 percent of the medium-sized ones, and 79 percent of the large ones have obtained business loans. Since the black-owned establishments tend to be smaller, this helps to explain why fewer blacks have borrowed for their businesses. But it does not fully explain the difference, for on every size level, the Harlem whites show a higher proportion of borrowers than the blacks. The Bay Ridge merchants, however, were more likely than blacks to have had loans only when their establishments were large. This can be seen from Table 4.11.

Those who had borrowed for business purposes were asked where they had obtained their last loan. Not only were the Harlem white merchants more likely to borrow money and to obtain a loan when they needed it, but they were also more likely to secure the loan through the established commercial source—namely, a bank. Ninety percent of the Harlem whites, 86 percent of the Bay Ridge merchants, and 70 percent of the Harlem blacks had obtained their loans from a bank. The remaining 30 percent of the blacks had turned to finance companies, to the Small Business Administration, or to friends and relatives.

Another question further documents the greater difficulty of the blacks in obtaining commercial loans. Regardless of whether they had borrowed before, all merchants were asked whether they had ever been refused a loan. Thirty-six percent of the blacks said they had, compared with 16 percent of the

Harlem whites.[6] On this matter, too, the merchants in the
Bay Ridge control group appear to have fewer problems than
the Harlem whites, for only 4 percent of them had ever been
refused a loan. A follow-up question revealed that almost all
of the loan rejections in both the white and black groups
were by banks.

Whereas the probability of having received a business loan
is positively related to size of firm, the probability of having
been refused a loan is negatively related to size. Of the small
businesses surveyed, 29 percent reported loan refusals; among
the medium-sized firms, the refusal rate was 17 percent; and
among the large firms it was 15 percent. Among the Harlem
whites the refusal rate progressively decreases as size of firm
increases, dropping from 21 percent to 18 percent to a low of
12 percent for the large firms. Among the blacks, the pattern
is curvilinear. Forty-two percent of the small-firm owners
reported loan refusals, 22 percent of those owning medium-
sized firms, and 36 percent of the large-firm owners. (For the
Bay Ridge sample, no pattern is evident, as too few of these
merchants had ever been refused a loan.) The discrepancy in
refusal rates between blacks and whites in Harlem is most
pronounced for the large firms. In this category only one
white in eight was turned away by a lending agency, whereas
one black in every three had this experience. Since the need
for loans is probably greatest for the large-store owner, this
finding reinforces the earlier evidence pointing to the
competitive disadvantage of the black merchants operating
large firms.

The businessman with established credit is likely to think
first of a bank as the source of a loan, since bank interest
rates are usually lower than those of other credit agencies.
The disadvantaged position of the blacks is further revealed
by the responses to a query about where the businessman
would seek a loan if he needed money now. Seventy-four
percent of the whites in Harlem said they would go to a
bank; and in Bay Ridge, this response was even more
frequent, 85 percent; but only 43 percent of the black

merchants said they would go to a bank. Blacks were more likely to mention the Small Business Administration, finance companies, or friends.

The data have shown that black merchants have more difficulty raising capital than their white counterparts for reasons other than the size of their establishments. A further possibility is that blacks have this problem because their businesses are not yet well established. Whether there is any merit to this reasoning can be seen from Table 4.12 which shows the frequency of loan refusals according to the number of years the merchant has been at his current location.

We have used years at current location as the indicator of the firm's age and stability. By reading down each column we find that within each sample refusal rates decline with age. But the rows of the table show that blacks have the highest refusal rate in each age of firm category, indicating that experience or business stability does not explain the black-white differential.

Several factors have been explored that might account for the greater difficulty of the blacks in obtaining business loans, but the search has not been very productive. The modest contribution of the tested variables to the understanding of the problem is overshadowed by the difference that persists between black and white merchants. Whether this reflects discrimination on the part of the lenders, or some factor that has not been considered, such as the success of the business, is not known. Whatever the reasons, it is clear that black businessmen have more difficulty than their white counterparts in raising capital.

Insurance Problems

Much has been written about the difficulty encountered by ghetto merchants in obtaining insurance as a consequence of the urban riots of the 1960s. The data indicate that insurance is indeed a problem for Harlem merchants, black and white alike, although black merchants are even less likely

TABLE 4.10

PERCENTAGE EXPRESSING AN INTEREST IN POOLING ORDERS, BY SIZE OF FIRM

| | Harlem Merchants | | | | Bay Ridge Merchants | |
| | Blacks | | Whites | | | |
Size of Firm	%	n	%	n	%	n
Small	56	(71)	30	(27)	44	(25)
Medium	57	(30)	19	(32)	70	(10)
Large	69	(16)	27	(41)	67	(9)

TABLE 4.11

PERCENTAGE WHO HAVE BORROWED FOR BUSINESS PURPOSES, BY SIZE OF ESTABLISHMENT

| | Harlem Merchants | | | | Bay Ridge Merchants | |
| | Blacks | | Whites | | | |
Size of Establishment	%	n	%	n	%	n
Small	46	(76)	50	(26)	42	(26)
Medium	53	(30)	70	(33)	53	(15)
Large	69	(16)	81	(41)	91	(11)

TABLE 4.12

PERCENTAGE REFUSED LOANS, BY NUMBER OF YEARS AT CURRENT LOCATION

| | Harlem Merchants | | | | Bay Ridge Merchants | |
| | Blacks | | Whites | | | |
Number of Years at Location	%	n	%	n	%	n
Under 3 years	48	(31)	28	(18)	6	(16)
3-10 years	34	(32)	23	(13)	8	(12)
10 or more years	28	(43)	10	(49)	0	(24)

to have coverage. Thus 24 percent of the black merchants have no insurance at all, compared with 12 percent of the Harlem whites.

As is evident from Table 4.13, Harlem whites are more likely than blacks to have each type of insurance.

Although Harlem white merchants are better protected than the blacks, they are not as well off in this respect as whites in Bay Ridge. Among the 53 Bay Ridge merchants interviewed, all but one had some kind of coverage. The differences become even greater when we take into account the number of different types of insurance. As can be seen from Table 4.14, the Harlem whites and especially the Bay Ridge merchants are much more likely than the blacks to have multiple policies.

Only 48 percent of the black merchants have more than one type of coverage, in contrast with 72 percent of the Harlem whites and 94 percent of the Bay Ridge merchants. Only one-third of the blacks have three or more policies while this is true for more than one-half the Harlem whites and almost nine-tenths of the Bay Ridge merchants. This disparity between Harlem merchants and those in the control group lends validity to the claim that ghetto merchants have more difficulty in obtaining insurance. We have already seen that the Harlem whites tend to have larger stores than either the blacks or the Bay Ridge merchants, and large stores presumably have more insurance coverage. That the Bay Ridge merchants are much better covered than the Harlem whites even though their stores are smaller emphasizes the insurance problem confronting ghetto businessmen.

Size of establishment is indeed related to insurance: 22 percent of the small stores, 14 percent of those of medium size, and only 4 percent of the large stores carry no insurance at all. Conversely, 53 percent of the small stores, 67 percent of the medium-sized ones, and 88 percent of the large ones have multiple policies. Since black-owned stores are smaller than those owned by whites, perhaps size accounts for the discrepancy in insurance coverage. Whether this is the case can be seen from Table 4.15.

TABLE 4.13
TYPE OF INSURANCE CARRIED (in percentages)

Type of Insurance	Harlem Merchants		Bay Ridge Merchants
	Blacks	Whites	
Liability	53	74	92
Fire	56	69	92
Plate glass	34	45	87
Theft	24	32	60
Riot	8	34	32
None	24	12	2
n	(121)	(104)	(53)

TABLE 4.14
NUMBER OF INSURANCE POLICIES HELD (in percentages)

Number of Policies	Harlem Merchants		Bay Ridge Merchants
	Blacks	Whites	
None	24	12	2
One	28	16	4
Two	15	20	8
Three or more	33	52	86
Total	100	100	100

TABLE 4.15
INSURANCE COVERAGE, BY SIZE OF ESTABLISHMENT

Size of Establishment	Harlem Merchants				Bay Ridge Merchants	
	Blacks		Whites			
	%	n	%	n	%	n
A. *Percentage with No Insurance*						
Small	31	(74)	14	(28)	4	(26)
Medium	20	(30)	15	(33)	0	(15)
Large	0	(16)	7	(43)	0	(12)
B. *Percentage with Two or More Policies*						
Small	41	(74)	58	(28)	89	(26)
Medium	52	(30)	64	(33)	100	(15)
Large	75	(16)	88	(43)	100	(12)

Reading down columns we see that size of business relates to insurance coverage especially for blacks. In Bay Ridge size makes little difference; almost all the businessmen there are covered by multiple policies. Table 4.15 shows that blacks are not so well protected as the Harlem whites even when size is held constant, with one exception. All of the black-owned large stores are covered, but a few (7 percent) of the white-owned large stores have no insurance at all. The whites are more likely not only to have some coverage, but also tend to have multiple policies on each size level. Size of establishment does explain some of the differential in coverage between Harlem blacks and whites, but not all of it, a finding which calls attention to another unmet need of black businessmen.

The merchants were asked if any of their insurance policies were cancelled in recent years. Further evidence of the ghetto insurance problem is provided by these data. Perhaps because they had more coverage initially, the Harlem whites were also more likely than blacks to report cancellations. Sixty-three percent of the whites, in contrast with 35 percent of the blacks, have had policies cancelled; in the middle-class Bay Ridge community, only 11 percent reported cancellations. The larger the store owned by blacks and whites in Harlem, the more frequent the reports of cancellation, although the pattern is somewhat irregular for the blacks. This is not too surprising since large stores are more likely to have insurance and multiple policies. Thus 44 percent of the large black-owned stores, 57 percent of those of medium size, and 24 percent of the small, experienced cancellations. For the Harlem whites, the comparable figures are 76, 71, and 35 percent.

The merchants were also asked whether they were having trouble getting insurance. The Harlem whites were somewhat more likely to respond affirmatively—60 percent compared with 53 percent for the blacks—but even in the control group, a substantial minority (43 percent) reported difficulty. Both the blacks and the whites of Harlem agreed that fire insurance was most difficult to obtain, followed by theft, and then by riot insurance.

We have already seen that the owners of large establishments were more likely to report cancellations. In each sample, the large stores were also more likely to have difficulty getting insurance, the figures for small and large black-owned stores being 51 percent and 60 percent; for Harlem whites, 60 and 65 percent; and for Bay Ridge merchants, 39 and 60 percent.

Those who did have some form of business insurance were asked whether the cost of insurance had risen in the past few years. A substantial majority in the three groups answered affirmatively: 81 percent of the Harlem whites, 73 percent of the Harlem blacks, and 72 percent of the Bay Ridge whites. That insurance costs have gone up for the Bay Ridge merchants indicates that the insurance rise is not limited to the ghetto community.

Those who carried insurance were also asked the total cost of their insurance per year. We have already noted that, on the average, the white merchants had more policies than the black merchants and therefore it comes as no surprise that whites pay substantially more. Some 61 percent of the Harlem whites who had insurance reported paying more than $600, compared with 30 percent of the blacks. In the control group, the proportion paying this much is even higher than for the Harlem whites, 72 percent. However, among those paying at least $1,000 per year for insurance, the Harlem whites are far ahead, with 51 percent paying at least this much, compared with 39 percent of the Bay Ridge merchants and only 19 percent of the black merchants.

To summarize, insurance is a pressing problem for both black and white merchants in Harlem. White merchants have more policies and also have had more cancellations. Almost all merchants with insurance have experienced rate increases. Owners of businesses with weak capital structures are apt to carry minimal insurance so as to maximize working capital. This, indeed, is more characteristic of the black merchants who were found to have less coverage or none at all, which means that they are extremely vulnerable to some business catastrophe.

Further Analysis of Business Problems

Three of the themes examined so far are central to the retail firm's capacity to survive and thrive: the ability to obtain supplies and merchandise on the most economical terms, to raise capital, and to obtain insurance. In comparing black and white merchants, we have seen a striking difference between the businessman's perception of problems in these areas and the extent of their actual existence. This was particularly true of relations with suppliers. Proportionately fewer blacks than whites recognize problems with suppliers. Nonetheless, analysis revealed that the blacks were more likely to buy from jobbers rather than from wholesalers or manufacturers, and they were more likely to pay C.O.D. We also saw that blacks were somewhat more likely to report that they had problems borrowing money but many more blacks than whites reported having been turned down for a loan. And in connection with insurance, we saw that the blacks had less coverage than the Harlem whites and yet were no more likely than the whites to report having trouble getting insurance. To explore this disparity between *perceived* or reported problems and what might be called *objective* problems, we have constructed indices of each of these phenomena. To measure the degree to which the businessman acknowledges problems in these areas, we have combined the responses to four questions, two of which deal with suppliers, one with raising capital and one with insurance. Scores of 1 were given to those who responded affirmatively to the direct question about problems with suppliers, getting credit from suppliers, raising capital for their business, and obtaining insurance for their business. When these scores are combined, the resulting index ranges from 0 to 4. Unfortunately, not all respondents answered all the questions that comprise this index. Some 80 percent answered four, 18 percent answered three and 1 percent answered two. (Two merchants answered only one of the questions and three did not answer any; these cases were excluded from the analysis.) Those who answered some of the questions were assigned a scale position on the basis of the questions that they did answer. This was somewhat easier to do when the five scale scores were condensed into three. Table 4.16 shows the distribution of merchants according to their scores on the condensed version of this index of *perceived* problems in the areas of supplies, capital and insurance.

The data show little difference between the two Harlem groups. The blacks are only slightly more likely to be in the "high" category on perceived problems, a finding that was to be expected on the basis of the previous analysis. Were we then to measure problems only on the basis of the merchants' readiness to report them, we would have to conclude that the whites in Harlem are almost as prone as the blacks to problems and that both groups have substantially more business problems than the merchants in the middle-class Bay Ridge control group.

Contrary to some earlier findings which have shown that size of firm is a cushion against difficulties, this index of reported problems shows a slight *positive* correlation with size. Thus, about one-quarter of the small and medium-sized firms score "high" on this index, but a third of the large firms do. This pattern holds also within each of the three samples. The large firms, whether they are black- or white-owned or located in Bay Ridge, are somewhat more likely than the small firms to be in the category of "high" perceived problems. This may be due in part to the association already examined between size and having diffi- culty obtaining insurance. It may also be due to the greater readiness of the large firms to try to raise capital.

To measure "objective" problems as distinct from reported problems, we have proceeded in a similar fashion, selecting items from the same three areas. However, this index is not completely comparable, for it is based on *five* items, two from the area of suppliers, one from the area of raising capital, and two from the insurance area. Those who bought *all* their supplies from jobbers were given a score of 1, as were those who *always* paid C.O.D. for merchandise. Those who had been refused a loan were also scored 1. (It should be noted that the inclusion of this item permits those who never applied for a loan to escape without a problem in this area.) From the insurance area, we have counted both those who reported that they have had policies cancelled and those who currently have no insurance at all. Again, not all the merchants answered these five questions, and we have followed a similar scoring procedure of assigning those who answered at least some of the questions to one of the three categories in the collapsed version according to the responses given. Table 4.17 shows the distribution of those in each sample in the condensed version of the index which includes those answering some of the questions.

Even though this index is based on five items and the other was based on four, we have collapsed it in the same way. The low category is comprised of those who had none of these problems, the medium category of those who had one, and the high category of those who had two or more. The somewhat greater proportion who are grouped in the high category when all the samples are combined is probably *not* an artifact of the index being based on five rather than four items. Thus for the Bay Ridge merchants and the Harlem whites, the proportion scoring high actually declines when we move from "reported problems" to "objective problems." The aggregate increase in the high category turns out to be due entirely to the blacks. On reported problems, shown in Table 4.16, only a third of the blacks are in the high category; but on this index of "objective" problems, more than half of them are so classified. Thus the very small difference between blacks and Harlem whites in Table 4.16 now increases substantially. This, of course, reflects what we have already learned. Black merchants buy their goods in a less economical way than the whites, they are more likely to have been turned down for loans, and are less likely to have insurance. Thus, whether they know it or not, they are more likely than the whites to have problems in the competitive marketplace. Table 4.17 also shows that the merchants in the control group have far fewer problems than the Harlem merchants, black or white.

The reported problem index and the objective problem index are, of course, related, but as Table 4.18 shows, (based on the aggregate of the three samples), the relationship is far from perfect.

Although reported problems tend to increase with objective problems, some 25 percent of those who are high on the objective index did not report any problems, and conversely, 10 percent of those in the low category on objective problems still reported several problems.

That these indices do not measure the same concept is shown by their connection with size of establishment. As noted, reported problems is *positively* related to size, with the large firms reporting more problems. But the objective problem index is *negatively* related to size, with the small firms scoring somewhat higher on the index than the large firms. Thus, 32 percent of all the small firms now fall into the high category compared with 28 percent of those of medium size and 23 percent of the large firms. This is not surprising as the objective index is based on having no insurance, dealing with jobbers only, and paying C.O.D. only; and it is the small firm that is likely to be totally without insurance and to buy in small quantities from jobbers and pay C.O.D. But this negative relationship with size does not hold within each ethnic group, as can be seen from Table 4.19.

The small black-owned stores have a much higher rate of problems than the stores in any other category. Moreover, among the blacks, objective problems decrease with size, whereas among the whites they tend to increase with size,

TABLE 4.16

DISTRIBUTION OF MERCHANTS ON INDEX OF PERCEIVED PROBLEMS (in percentages)

Score on Index of Perceived Problems	Harlem Merchants Blacks	Whites	Bay Ridge Merchants	Total (All Samples)
Low (0)	29	32	43	33
Medium (1)	38	39	47	40
High (2, 3, 4)	33	29	9	27
Total	100	100	99	100
n	(123)	(106)	(53)	(282)

TABLE 4.17

DISTRIBUTION OF MERCHANTS ON INDEX OF "OBJECTIVE" PROBLEMS (in percentages)

Score on Index of Objective Problems	Harlem Merchants Blacks	Whites	Bay Ridge Merchants	Total (All Samples)
Low (0)	11	25	72	28
Medium (1)	37	49	21	38
High (2, 3, 4, 5)	52	26	7	34
Total	100	100	100	100
n	(123)	(105)	(53)	(281)

TABLE 4.18

PERCEIVED PROBLEMS BY OBJECTIVE PROBLEMS (three samples combined) (in percentages)

Reported Problems	Objective Problems Low	Medium	High
Low	53	25	25
Medium	37	46	36
High	10	29	39
Total	100	100	100
n	(78)	(108)	(95)

and among Bay Ridge merchants the pattern tends to be curvilinear as the stores of medium size score higher than the small and large ones. By comparing the groups, we learn that the Harlem whites with small stores are much less likely to score high on problems than the blacks with small stores, and that in the medium-sized category, the whites are also more likely to be problem-free. But among the large stores, those owned by whites are slightly *more* likely to be in the high-problem category than those owned by blacks. This is somewhat surprising, for we have seen earlier that the large black-owned stores have less efficient relationships with suppliers than do those owned by whites, but the whites were more likely to have experienced insurance cancellation in this size category.

How does type of business relate to the objective problem index? Will the differences between Harlem whites and blacks disappear when type of business is taken into account? The answer is provided in Table 4.20. Since hardly any Bay Ridge merchants score high on the index, we have excluded them from this table.

Table 4.20 makes it quite clear that the blacks are more beset with problems than the whites. In every type of business, black merchants are more likely to be in the high category. The difference is particularly pronounced in the stores merchandising high-cost items.

It is conceivable that a merchant's score on the objective problem index is related not only to the size of his store and the type of his business, but also to the amount of training and preparation he has had for a business career. Table 4.21 relates the objective problem index to the measure of business background developed in Chapter 2.

Table 4.21 is quite startling for it shows that the blacks apparently do benefit from their business experience in that the more experience they have, the less likely they are to be in the high-problem category. But among the whites, the opposite relationship holds. The stronger the white merchant's business background, the *more* likely he is to be beset

TABLE 4.19

PERCENTAGE SCORING HIGH ON OBJECTIVE PROBLEMS, BY SIZE OF ESTABLISHMENT

| | Harlem Merchants | | | | Bay Ridge Merchants | |
| | Blacks | | Whites | | | |
Size of Establishment	%	n	%	n	%	n
Small	61	(76)	14	(28)	8	(26)
Medium	47	(30)	29	(34)	13	(15)
Large	25	(16)	30	(43)	0	(12)

TABLE 4.20

PERCENTAGE OF BLACK AND WHITE MERCHANTS IN HARLEM SCORING HIGH ON OBJECTIVE PROBLEMS, BY TYPE OF BUSINESS

| Harlem Sample | Automotive Services | | Other Services | | Low-Cost Items | | High-Cost Items | |
	%	n	%	n	%	n	%	n
Blacks	39	(13)	56	(41)	47	(45)	63	(24)
Whites	13	(8)	42	(19)	24	(41)	22	(37)

TABLE 4.21

PERCENTAGE OF BLACK AND WHITE MERCHANTS IN HARLEM SCORING HIGH ON OBJECTIVE PROBLEMS, BY BUSINESS BACKGROUND INDEX

| | Harlem Merchants | | | |
| | Blacks | | Whites | |
Business Background Index	%	n	%	n
Weak	61	(59)	12	(25)
Moderate	49	(41)	20	(55)
Strong	32	(22)	52	(25)

with problems. It is possible that this relationship is spurious, for we already know that the white owners of large establishments have more business experience and they are also more likely to have the kinds of problems captured in this index than are the whites who own small stores. Nonetheless, it would seem that training and experience in business does have a pay-off for the blacks in that those who score high on business background are not nearly so likely to have problems as those whose business background is weak. Why the reverse holds for the whites is not known, but it is difficult to conceive of the white pattern as a causal one; that is, that familiarity with business produces problems. Most likely such intervening variables as size or type of business explain the pattern for the whites.

In Chapter 3 we classified businessmen according to their record-keeping practices. Presumably the businessman who keeps accurate records is a better businessman than the one who does not, and if attention to detail is an antidote to problems, then we should find that those who keep good records have fewer problems than those who do not. But again the data belie this reasoning (Table 4.22).

Skill in keeping records is clearly no antidote to problems, for among both the blacks and whites in Harlem, those who score poorly on record-keeping have fewer objective problems than those who score well on this index. It is hardly likely that keeping good records causes the types of problems captured in our index and thus these results must be an artifact of other variables associated with record-keeping, such as size and type of establishment.

Security Problems and Riot Experience

The final theme to be explored in this chapter concerns security problems. All the merchants were asked questions about theft and pilferage and the Harlem merchants were asked, in addition, whether their stores had been damaged during the riots that had taken place in the sixties. White merchants of Harlem were more prone than blacks to report that shoplifting was a major problem for them (45 percent versus 27 percent). This is not altogether surprising since white merchants sell more expensive items whereas black merchants deal more in low-cost items or in service-type establishments. In the control group, 23 percent (about the same as the Harlem blacks) answered this question affirmatively.

In addition to customer theft, storekeepers worry about employee stealing. Incidence of employee stealing is apparently less serious in these samples. When asked directly about this issue, only 14 percent of the blacks, 19 percent of the Harlem whites, and 16 percent of those in the control group said that this was a problem.

Two further items dealt with security: the frequency of burglaries and holdups. The reputation of the ghetto community is such that burglaries and holdups of merchants are assumed to be quite common. With regard to burglaries, 53 percent of the blacks and 55 percent of the whites in Harlem reported having been burglarized in the past two years, while in Bay Ridge 29 percent reported burglaries. It is to be noted that the burglary rate is about the same for blacks and whites in Harlem and that even in the more middle-class community of Bay Ridge, burglaries occur with appreciable frequency.

On the matter of holdups, the whites in Harlem are more likely than the blacks to have had this experience at least once during the past two years: 30 percent compared with 17 percent. The holdup rate in Bay Ridge is similar to that of the Harlem blacks, 16 percent. In each group a majority of those who had this experience had it only once, but in keeping with their initially higher rate, the whites in Harlem were somewhat more likely than the blacks to have experienced multiple holdups: 12 percent compared with 7 percent; for the Bay Ridge merchants, the rate is 8 percent.

It is quite likely that the merchants who have been burglarized were also more likely to have been held up and thus, to provide a more accurate picture of the security problems of the merchants in our samples, we have combined both questions into what might be called a "larceny victim" typology. Table 4.23 compares the three samples in this respect.

Table 4.23 verifies the greater hazards confronting ghetto merchants. Whereas 61 percent of the Bay Ridge merchants escaped both experiences, this was true of only 42 percent of the blacks and 37 percent of the Harlem whites.

Whether the businessman has these security problems is related to the size of his establishment, but most interestingly, this relationship is positive for the blacks and the Bay Ridge merchants, but negative for the Harlem whites, as can be seen from Table 4.24.

Among blacks, the pattern tends to be curvilinear in that the highest larceny-victim rate is found in the medium-sized stores, but the key point is that the small black-owned businesses have the lowest rate, whereas among the whites, the small stores have the highest rate. This reversal is particularly evident if we consider the data on holdups only. Among blacks, the holdup rate increases from 14 percent to 24 percent to 30 percent as we move from small to medium to large stores; whereas among the Harlem whites, the holdup rate *declines* from 38 percent to 35 percent to 21 percent as size of store increases. As a result, in the large stores, the blacks show a higher rate of holdups than the whites. This difference in the patterning of the security problem for blacks and whites in Harlem may be a reflection of the different locations of the large black- and white-owned firms. We have already seen that some 35 percent of the white-owned businesses are located on the busiest and presumably the best-policed thoroughfare in Harlem—125th Street. To test this hypothesis fully, we would have to control simultaneously for size and location within each ethnic group, but we have too few cases for such a refined test. Nonetheless, the role of location in this pattern can be seen from Table 4.25.

Among blacks, the probability of being the victim of

TABLE 4.22
PERCENTAGE OF BLACK AND WHITE HARLEM MERCHANTS SCORING HIGH ON OBJECTIVE PROGLEMS, BY RECORD-KEEPING INDEX

| | Harlem Merchants | | | |
| | Blacks | | Whites | |
Record-Keeping Behavior	%	n	%	n
Poor	19	(21)	16	(19)
Medium	37	(74)	32	(69)
Good	33	(27)	33	(18)

TABLE 4.23
A COMPARISON OF THE THREE SAMPLES, ACCORDING TO "LARCENY VICTIM" TYPOLOGY (in percentages)

| | Harlem Merchants | | Bay Ridge |
Larceny Victim	Blacks	Whites	Merchants
Neither burglarized nor held up	42	37	61
Burglarized only	40	33	23
Held up only	5	8	2
Both held up and burglarized	13	22	14
Total	100	100	100
n	(124)	(106)	(51)

TABLE 4.24
PERCENTAGE WHO HAVE BEEN VICTIMS OF LARCENY, ACCORDING TO SIZE OF ESTABLISHMENT

| | Harlem Merchants | | | | Bay Ridge | |
| | Blacks | | Whites | | Merchants | |
Size of Establishment	%	n	%	n	%	n
Small	49	(76)	76	(29)	32	(25)
Medium	80	(30)	59	(34)	36	(14)
Large	65	(17)	58	(43)	58	(12)

larceny is virtually the same, whatever the location, but for whites store location is apparently related to security. White merchants located on the well-traveled and well-policed 125th Street are less likely to be victims of larceny than those located on the major avenues, and the latter in turn are less likely to be victimized than those on the minor avenues.

Harlem was the scene of at least two major riots between 1964 and 1968. The last, sparked by the death of Dr. Martin Luther King, occurred shortly before the field work for this survey began. The Harlem merchants were asked whether their store had been damaged during any of these disturbances. A noticeable difference is to be found between black and white merchants in this respect. More than one-third of the whites, 35 percent, reported damage to their stores as a result of riots compared with 14 percent of the blacks. The presumed selectivity of rioters has frequently been reported, and this finding would suggest that such selectivity was at work in Harlem. But before accepting this conclusion, we must remember that a much larger proportion of the white merchants are located on the street that carried the brunt of the rioting, 125th Street. Whether location in any way explains the black-white differential in riot damage can be seen from Table 4.26.

Table 4.26 lends much support to the hypothesis of selectivity, for the white-owned stores were more likely to have been damaged whatever their location. Moreover, Table 4.26 casts doubt on the notion that the 125th Street merchants were most likely to have suffered in the riots. Among the whites, we find similar proportions reporting riot damage at the different locations; in fact, the highest rate is found among whites located on the minor avenues.

Summary

A number of problems confronting ghetto merchants have been explored. Both Harlem merchants and those in the middle-class control group were likely to complain about

TABLE 4.25
PERCENTAGE WHO HAVE BEEN VICTIMS OF LARCENY AMONG HARLEM BLACKS AND WHITES, ACCORDING TO LOCATION

	Harlem Merchants			
	Blacks		Whites	
Location	%	n	%	n
125th Street	60	(5)	57	(37)
Major avenues	58	(93)	65	(48)
Minor avenues and 116th Street	58	(26)	71	(21)

TABLE 4.26
PERCENTAGE REPORTING RIOT DAMAGE, AMONG HARLEM BLACKS AND WHITES, ACCORDING TO LOCATION

	Harlem Merchants			
	Blacks		Whites	
Location of Store	%	n	%	n
125th Street	25	(4)	35	(37)
Major avenues	11	(92)	33	(48)
Minor avenues and 116th Street	23	(26)	40	(20)

personnel problems, with the blacks being even more likely
to have this problem than the Harlem whites. For the ghetto
merchants, the personnel problem was largely a matter of
finding reliable employees with the requisite skills; for the
Bay Ridge merchants, the problem was one of finding people
willing to work in retail establishments, indicating the very
different labor markets available to ghetto merchants and
those in a middle-class area.

Potential problems with suppliers were explored and it was
found that the blacks were more likely to deal with jobbers
than with wholesalers and manufacturers, a finding only
partly explained by their stores being smaller. Not only did
blacks deal more frequently with the less economical
suppliers, but they were much less likely to get credit from
their suppliers, having to pay C.O.D. for their merchandise
more frequently than the Harlem whites and the Bay Ridge
merchants.

The Harlem merchants, both black and white, had more
difficulty borrowing money for business purposes than the
merchants in the control group, but the blacks had this
problem more frequently than the Harlem whites. Thus the
blacks were less likely to have ever borrowed, more likely to
have been refused loans, and less likely to have obtained
loans from the banks, the most economical source of capital.
Just as differences with suppliers could not be explained by
size and type of business, so the greater advantage of the
Harlem whites in obtaining loans could not be fully explained
by these factors.

The widely held belief that ghetto merchants have more
difficulty getting insurance was well supported by the data.
Both blacks and whites in Harlem were less likely to be
covered by insurance than the whites in the control group,
and those who were covered had fewer policies. The Harlem
merchants were more likely to report cancellations of
insurance and were more likely to have had difficulties
getting insurance. In all these respects the blacks were worse
off than the Harlem whites, with more totally without
insurance and with fewer policies.

We saw that the Harlem merchants, both black and white, had more security problems than those in the Bay Ridge sample and that in Harlem the whites were even more vulnerable than the blacks. We also saw that the Harlem whites were more likely to have suffered property destruction from the recent riots, confirming the selectivity hypothesis.

A distinction was made between perceived problems and objective problems confronting the merchants. The blacks were more likely to have problems in the areas of obtaining merchandise, raising capital, and getting insurance than they themselves recognized or, at least, were ready to report. The differences between blacks and whites in these respects persisted when size and type of establishment were held constant. Having reviewed the problems of Harlem merchants, we turn in the next chapter to an analysis of their success in business.

Chapter 5

THE ECONOMIC HEALTH OF HARLEM BUSINESSES

This chapter assesses the success or economic health of black- and white-owned businesses. It was impractical to ask these businessmen to show us their books or furnish exact figures on their profits or losses. But we could ask them: (1) to compare the current state of their business relative to the previous year; (2) whether they had made or lost money in the year just completed; and (3) whether the previous year was an improvement over the one before that. Indicators such as these provide crude measures of the profitability of the business. They tell us whether things are getting better or worse for the businessmen and thus measure what might be called *relative* success or failure. We shall also look at the data on *gross* sales as a crude measure of *absolute* success. Of course, it is quite possible that the firm with a large volume of sales is actually losing money or is declining, but by the same token, the probability is quite high that the firm with large gross sales is profiting more than the one with very small gross sales. Certainly, merchants whose gross sales are less than $10,000 cannot possibly be making much money, and although businessmen with gross sales of a quarter-of-a-million dollars may not be making a great deal of money, the chances are that the profits of those in the latter category are greater than those in the former. Still a third measure of "success" will be examined, one that is much more indirect, namely, whether the businessman plans to stay in business at his current location, relocate, or sell his business. We shall begin with an analysis of the data on gross sales—our crude measure of absolute success.

Gross Sales

It will be recalled from the first chapter that gross sales was one of the three indicators used to measure the size of the establishment, along with number of employees and square feet of space occupied by the store. At that time we pointed out the sharp disparity between blacks and whites with respect to gross sales, noting that about one-half the whites reported sales in excess of $100,000 in contrast with only 16 percent of the blacks. The difference in gross sales between blacks and whites in Harlem is even sharper than these figures indicate. Table 5.1 presents a detailed break-down of gross sales for merchants in all three groups. It should be noted that these figures are based only on those who answered the question. Some 18 percent of the Harlem blacks, 23 percent of the Harlem whites, and more than one-third of the Bay Ridge merchants refused to disclose their annual gross sales.

From Table 5.1 we see that more than half the black businessmen had gross sales under $25,000 in contrast with 21 percent of the Harlem whites and 24 percent of the Bay Ridge merchants. At the other extreme, only 16 percent of the blacks had gross sales of over $100,000 compared with 51 percent of the whites and 41 percent of the Bay Ridge merchants. Both the mean and median for each sample were computed from these grouped data. In carrying out the computations, the mid-point for each interval was used except for the lowest category where it was arbitrarily assumed that the mid-point was $4,000 rather than $2,500. The disparity between the Harlem blacks and whites is made quite vivid from these figures. The mean for the blacks is $46,333. For the whites, it is two-and-one-half times as high: $109,700. The distribution for blacks is more skewed than that for whites, and hence the median for the blacks is significantly lower than the mean. The median among the blacks is only $22,143, and for the whites it is almost five times higher: $103,846. These figures make amply clear that however close the proportions of black- and white-owned establishments in Harlem are, the whites account for substantially more gross sales than the blacks. Even though only 82 whites answered this question, their gross sales totaled approximately $9,000,000. In contrast, the 102 blacks who responded had in the aggregate under $5,000,000 gross sales.

From Table 5.1 we learn also that the gross sales of the Harlem whites substantially exceed those of the Bay Ridge merchants. The latter fall between the Harlem whites and blacks although they are closer to the whites.

Do the differences in gross sales between blacks and whites merely reflect the tendency of the whites to own larger stores? To answer this question we cannot use the size index already developed for it includes gross sales as one of its dimensions. Thus for this analysis of gross sales we have constructed a separate size index comprised of the other two items, the number of employees, and the number of square feet of floor space. (We shall use this two-item index of size throughout this section.) Table 5.2 compares the three samples on median gross sales in each size category.

The data for the Bay Ridge sample are less reliable since so many of the Bay Ridge merchants, particularly those owning small stores, failed to supply information on gross sales. In each sample, gross sales, of course, increase with size. More important, however, Table 5.2 shows that the Harlem whites

have larger gross sales than the blacks even when size of
establishment is held constant. The difference between the
two groups, though narrow in the small stores, increases
substantially in the stores of medium and large size. Black
owners of even large stores do far less business than white
owners of stores of medium size.

Table 5.3 compares the three samples with respect to gross
sales when type of business is held constant.

We have already noted that the Bay Ridge data on gross
sales are less reliable since fully 36 percent of the merchants
in that sample did not respond. Table 5.3 raises some more
questions about the Bay Ridge sample. The automotive
services in Bay Ridge report by far the highest gross sales in
that community; in fact the median for this group is higher
than that of any other store type in any of the samples. Even
more amazingly, the nine Bay Ridge merchants selling
high-cost items who answered this question have the lowest
median gross sales of any group, only $8,750. This is difficult
to believe for included here are three furniture stores, one
furniture upholstery establishment, and five appliance stores.
A closer examination shows that five of these nine Bay Ridge
stores are small in size and their median gross sales is only
$4,833. The 20 black-owned high-cost-item stores also have a
low median gross sales, only $15,000 (the lowest among the
blacks). The black stores in this category are more heterogeneous: four of them sell tires and auto accessories, six sell
radios and TV sets, three are jewelry stores, two sell
furniture, two are shoe stores, and two sell women's
accessories. Only among the Harlem whites do the gross sales
of the high-cost-item stores correspond to expectations.
These stores have the highest median in the white sample
($130,000).

Table 5.3 makes quite clear that the disparity between
blacks and whites cannot be explained by store type, for in
every type of business, the median gross sales of the Harlem
whites is higher. Only in automotive services do blacks come
close to whites in gross sales. This group constitutes the

TABLE 5.1
DISTRIBUTION OF MERCHANTS ACCORDING TO
GROSS SALES IN 1967 (in percentages)

Gross Sales	Harlem Merchants		Bay Ridge Merchants
	Blacks	Whites	
Under $25,000	56	21	24
$25,000-$99,999	28	28	35
$100,000-$250,000	16	51	41
Total	100	100	100
n	(102)	(82)	(34)
Mean Sales	$46,333	$109,700	$91,176
Median Sales	$22,143	$103,846	$75,000

TABLE 5.2
MEDIAN GROSS SALES, BY SIZE OF ESTABLISHMENT

Size of Establishment	Harlem Merchants				Bay Ridge Merchants	
	Blacks		Whites			
	$	n	$	n	$	n
Small	14,167	(49)	17,500	(15)	10,000	(10)
Medium	48,216	(41)	125,000	(35)	81,250	(15)
Large	75,000	(12)	141,667	(32)	160,000	(9)

TABLE 5.3
MEDIAN GROSS SALES, BY TYPE OF BUSINESS

Type of Business	Harlem Merchants				Bay Ridge Merchants	
	Blacks		Whites			
	$	n	$	n	$	n
Automotive services	45,833	(11)	50,000	(6)	137,500	(6)
Other services	22,500	(33)	87,500	(15)	72,500	(4)
Low-cost items	22,000	(38)	72,917	(33)	79,167	(15)
High-cost items	15,000	(20)	130,000	(28)	8,750	(9)

highest median sales among blacks, but the lowest among whites. In the other categories, the median of whites is three to nine times higher than that of blacks. These results are a reminder of the heterogeneity within our broad categories of store types. Ideally, we would want to compare black- and white-owned stores selling the same items or providing the same services but we have too few cases for this more refined comparison. In the subsequent analysis of gross sales we shall hold size of store constant rather than type since size shows the same relationship to gross sales within each sample and is less ambiguous.

That the whites in Harlem have larger gross sales than the blacks might be due in part to the fact that they have been in business longer and are more established. To test this possibility, years at current location are related to gross sales, within each category of size (Table 5.4). Since this analysis involves looking at four variables simultaneously (ethnicity as well), the relatively small number of Bay Ridge merchants will be ignored.

By reading the rows of the table we find that, contrary to expectation, length of time at current location is unrelated to gross sales. In fact, the stores that have been at their location only a few years are apt to report higher gross sales than those that have been there longer. We have used length of time at current location as an indicator of how well established the enterprise is in the community, but these data suggest another interpretation. It may very well be that the more successful stores have moved to larger quarters and thus do not have much tenure at their current location. In short, this variable may be less a measure of business experience than it is of business expansion and growth. Table 5.4 also permits us to make nine comparisons between black and white merchants; in all but one, the whites report higher gross sales. The ethnic difference is particularly marked in the firms of medium size. The one exception occurs in the large stores that have been at their current location for less than three years. There are only two black-owned stores in this

TABLE 5.4

MEDIAN GROSS SALES FOR HARLEM BLACKS
AND WHITES, BY YEARS AT CURRENT LOCATION,
WITH SIZE OF FIRM HELD CONSTANT

Size of Firm	Years at Current Location					
	Under 3		3-9		10 or More	
	$	n	$	n	$	n
Small						
Blacks	19,000	(14)	11,875	(15)	13,750	(20)
Whites	22,500	(4)	15,000	(4)	20,000	(7)
Medium						
Blacks	41,667	(14)	31,250	(10)	59,375	(16)
Whites	125,000	(6)	52,875	(4)	135,000	(25)
Large						
Blacks	106,250	(2)	87,500	(10)	62,500	(7)
Whites	100,000	(8)	192,857	(8)	112,500	(16)

TABLE 5.5

MEDIAN GROSS SALES FOR HARLEM BLACKS
AND WHITES, BY STRENGTH OF BUSINESS BACKGROUND,
WITH SIZE OF FIRM HELD CONSTANT

Size of Firm	Business Background					
	Weak		Moderate		Strong	
	$	n	$	n	$	n
Small						
Blacks	11,667	(28)	18,000	(15)	46,875	(6)
Whites	15,000	(12)	37,500	(3)	—	(0)
Medium						
Blacks	41,667	(18)	43,750	(13)	56,250	(9)
Whites	103,750	(2)	125,000	(25)	145,834	(6)
Large						
Blacks	41,250	(2)	166,667	(5)	20,000	(5)
Whites	75,000	(8)	160,000	(18)	145,834	(6)

category and their average gross sales is somewhat higher than that of the eight white-owned stores of this type.

To what extent is training or preparation for business, as measured by the index developed in Chapter 2, related to "absolute" success, that is gross sales? These data are shown in Table 5.5 which again deals only with Harlem merchants.

The relationship between business background and gross sales can be seen from the rows of the table. There are six rows in all, and in five of them strength of business background does show some relationship to gross sales. The exception occurs in the large black-owned stores, where those with a moderate business background have far higher gross sales than those with either a strong or weak business background. Comparing blacks and whites, we again find that the gross sales of the whites exceed those of the blacks in every category except one, the owners of large stores who have a moderate score on business background. In this group, the blacks do slightly better than the whites.

Does keeping good financial records have a pay-off for the businessman's gross sales? The answer is provided by Table 5.6. The notion that keeping good records might somehow stimulate gross sales or even that the merchant with large sales is forced to keep good records finds limited support from the table. In only three of the six rows do we find some evidence for this relationship, the small white-owned stores and the large stores owned by whites and by blacks. And when both size and record-keeping are held constant, the whites in almost every instance have higher gross sales than the blacks. This time the exception occurs in the small stores with a poor score on record-keeping. Here the blacks have a slightly higher median than the whites.

Finally, we consider the impact of the types of problems that were reviewed in the previous chapter on gross sales, beginning with the index of objective problems, based on less economical methods of buying supplies, being refused a business loan, and insurance problems. These data are shown in Table 5.7.

TABLE 5.6

MEDIAN GROSS SALES OF HARLEM BLACKS AND WHITES, BY SCORE ON RECORD-KEEPING INDEX, WITH SIZE OF FIRM HELD CONSTANT

| | Record-Keeping Index | | | | | |
| | Poor | | Fair | | Good | |
Size of Firm	$	n	$	n	$	n
Small						
Blacks	13,750	(11)	15,833	(26)	13,125	(11)
Whites	10,000	(6)	37,500	(8)	62,500	(1)
Medium						
Blacks	43,750	(5)	49,531	(34)	20,000	(1)
Whites	175,000	(6)	112,500	(23)	145,834	(6)
Large						
Blacks	—	(0)	22,500	(3)	112,500	(9)
Whites	116,667	(5)	125,000	(22)	166,667	(5)

TABLE 5.7

MEDIAN GROSS SALES OF HARLEM BLACKS AND WHITES, BY OBJECTIVE PROBLEM INDEX, WITH SIZE OF FIRM HELD CONSTANT

| | Objective Problems Index | | | | | |
| | Low | | Medium | | High | |
Size of Firm	$	n	$	n	$	n
Small						
Blacks	62,500	(1)	13,000	(16)	14,938	(32)
Whites	22,500	(5)	7,500	(7)	56,250	(3)
Medium						
Blacks	37,500	(6)	46,875	(19)	53,125	(15)
Whites	56,250	(9)	137,500	(16)	150,833	(10)
Large						
Blacks	12,500	(1)	75,000	(8)	125,000	(3)
Whites	166,667	(5)	131,250	(19)	143,750	(8)

Contrary to what might have been expected, merchants who are free from problems tend to have lower gross sales than merchants who have the types of problems measured by this index. Thus in four of the six rows we find those who score high on objective problems with higher gross sales than those who score low. The results in the first row are inconclusive since there is only one small black-owned store that is low on problems. Only among the large white-owned establishments do the problem-free stores do better than those scoring high on problems. Clearly then, the types of business problems we have reviewed do not depress gross sales. On the contrary, the merchant who does a large volume of business is apt to have more problems, perhaps because insurance is more important to him and he is more apt to want to borrow money.

Again we find that the whites exceed the blacks in gross sales when other variables are held constant. The one clear reversal occurs in the small stores that score in the middle category on problems. Here blacks report higher gross sales than the whites. (We can ignore the other apparent reversal, the small stores that are low on problems, since there is only one black-owned establishment in this category and its sales happen to exceed the median of the five white-owned stores in this category.)

To summarize, white merchants in Harlem register sub-stantially higher gross sales than do black businessmen. We have tried to account for this difference in a number of ways, such as size of the business, type of business, years at current location, business experience, the degree of attention paid to keeping records, and the number of problems confronting the business. In every instance, the differences between blacks and whites on gross sales remained when these other variables were taken into account. In short, the whites of Harlem tend to have larger gross sales even when factors conducive to "success" are held constant. Perhaps it is the combination of the various advantages of whites that accounts for this difference. We have examined gross sales in such detail on the assumption that it is a crude measure of "absolute" success. We turn now to a consideration of *relative* success.

Relative Success

Merchants were asked three questions concerning the profitability of their business. The first dealt with whether they had made money, lost money, or had broken even in 1967 (the year prior to the survey). The second asked them to compare 1967 with 1966; the third asked about prospects for the current year (1968) in comparison with 1967. An interesting pattern emerges when these questions are examined. The white businessmen in Harlem are more likely to be making money, but the black businessmen are more likely to see their businesses as improving. And, oddly enough, the control group of Bay Ridge merchants conforms more to the pattern of the blacks in that they are least likely to have made money in 1967, but nonetheless see their business as improving with time. These patterns are shown in Table 5.8.

From part A of Table 5.8, we see that two-thirds of the white merchants in Harlem made a profit in 1967 compared with 44 percent of the blacks and only 40 percent of the control group. Substantially more of the blacks and Bay Ridge merchants than Harlem whites viewed 1967 as an improvement over 1966. And both groups report more success in 1968 than Harlem whites. The pattern for the Bay Ridge merchants is puzzling, whereas the patterns for the Harlem merchants tend to make sense considering that the blacks are more recent arrivals to the world of business and that their businesses tend to be smaller than those of the whites. In the opinion of the overwhelming majority of both black and white merchants in Harlem, the area in which their stores are located has deteriorated in the past year. (Seventy-three percent of the blacks and 76 percent of the whites were of this opinion.) When asked to explain why, many in both groups perceived a decline in the socio-economic status of the residents. With this in mind, we may conjecture that Harlem is becoming a less suitable location for merchants who have relatively expensive merchandise to sell. The relatively large and older white-owned establishment in these circumstances might well be experiencing a decline relative to the newer and smaller black-owned businesses. Whether this is in fact the case will be considered shortly when we examine the correlates of *relative* success.

There is one further item that bears on the merchants' estimates of how well they are doing, a question that asked them how worried they were that their business might fail. They could respond by saying they were very worried, somewhat worried, or not at all worried. In spite of their being more likely to have made a profit in the preceding year, the whites in Harlem were slightly more worried than the blacks that their business might fail. Some 15 percent of them said they were *very* worried about failing, compared with 12 percent of the blacks. At the other extreme, 73 percent of the blacks were *not at all* worried, compared with 68 percent of the whites. Again, the Bay Ridge control group proves to be somewhat of an enigma for, in spite of their being the group with the lowest proportion reporting a profit in 1967, they are least worried about business failure. Only 6 percent were *very* worried on this score, and 79 percent were *not at all* worried.

The three comparative items reported in Table 5.8 and the question concerning worry about failure have been combined into an index of what might be called *relative success* or optimism about the business. As can be seen from Table 5.9, blacks compare quite favorably with both the Harlem and Bay Ridge whites on this index.

There is little difference among the three samples; what difference there is indicates that Harlem blacks are relatively *more* successful or at least more optimistic than Harlem whites. What accounts for the fact that the blacks, in spite of their much smaller gross sales, score higher on this index of relative success? We shall first consider the relationship between this index and gross sales.

Table 5.10 shows the median gross sales for merchants on each level of relative success in each of the three samples, and the same relationship when all three samples are combined.

TABLE 5.8
INDICATORS OF STATUS OF BUSINESS (in percentages)

| | Harlem Merchants | | Bay Ridge |
	Black	White	Merchants
A. *1967 Profits*			
Made money	44	66	40
Broke even	37	23	46
Lost money	19	11	15
Total	100	100	101
n	(114)	(97)	(48)
B. *1966-1967 Relative Profits*			
Did better in 1967	43	29	44
About the same	37	47	37
Did better in 1966	20	24	19
Total	100	100	100
n[a]	(106)	(87)	(43)
C. *1967-1968 Relative Profits*			
Doing better in 1968	50	38	50
About the same	32	36	34
Did better in 1967	18	27	16
Total	100	101	100
n[a]	(112)	(90)	(44)

a. That fewer answered the second question than the first is due in part to the fact that some of these businesses did not exist in 1966. The smaller response rate to C is explained by the fact that some merchants were unable to estimate the outcome of the current year.

TABLE 5.9
RELATIVE BUSINESS SUCCESS (in percentages)

| Score on Index of Relative Success | Harlem Businessmen | | Bay Ridge Businessmen |
	Black	White	
Low	13	16	13
Medium low	21	19	21
Medium high	30	34	36
High	36	31	30
Total	100	100	100
n	(122)	(104)	(53)

From the last column of Table 5.10 we learn that in the aggregate there is a fairly strong positive relationship between relative success and gross sales. This aggregate pattern holds for the Harlem whites and for the Bay Ridge sample, but it does *not* hold for the Harlem blacks. True, the blacks who score medium high or high on relative success have higher gross sales than the blacks in the two lower categories of relative success, but the blacks who score medium high on relative success have far higher gross sales than those who score high. And whether the blacks are low or medium low on relative success has little bearing on their gross sales. The import of Table 5.10 is that the standards of relative success are different for the blacks and the whites. The blacks who judge their business as doing well are less attuned to gross sales than are the whites of Harlem and Bay Ridge.

The impact of size of firm on relative success in each sample can be seen from Table 5.11. In this table our standard measure of size is used which includes gross sales as well as number of employees and physical size of establishment. The figures in the table report those in each sample who score high on relative success; that is, those in the top category of success shown in the previous table.

Only in the Bay Ridge sample is there a clear positive relationship between size and relative success. Among the Harlem whites size makes some difference in that the smallest firms are least likely to be high on relative success, but the large firms do not do as well as those of medium size. The blacks show a contrasting pattern with the medium-sized firms exhibiting the lowest percentage.

The connection between type of business and relative success is shown in Table 5.12. From the last column showing the combined samples, we see that stores classified as Other Services are most likely to score high on relative success, but on closer inspection this finding is due mainly to the blacks in this type of business. When Harlem blacks and whites are compared, we find that their relative position on

TABLE 5.10
MEDIAN GROSS SALES BY RELATIVE SUCCESS

Relative Success	Harlem Merchants Blacks $	n	Whites $	n	Bay Ridge Merchants $	n	Total (All Samples) $	n
Low	17,000	(12)	28,750	(12)	37,500	(3)	19,167	(27)
Medium low	17,143	(23)	68,750	(14)	43,750	(7)	25,938	(44)
Medium high	53,125	(28)	125,000	(29)	68,750	(13)	69,231	(70)
High	25,831	(38)	160,000	(27)	131,250	(11)	65,000	(76)

TABLE 5.11
PERCENTAGE SCORING HIGH ON RELATIVE SUCCESS, BY SIZE OF ESTABLISHMENT

Size of Establishment	Harlem Merchants Blacks %	n	Whites %	n	Bay Ridge Merchants %	n	Total (All Samples) %	n
Small	39	(75)	11	(28)	15	(26)	28	(129)
Medium	30	(30)	47	(34)	40	(15)	39	(79)
Large	38	(16)	31	(42)	50	(12)	36	(70)

TABLE 5.12
PERCENTAGE HIGH ON RELATIVE SUCCESS, BY TYPE OF BUSINESS

Type of Business	Harlem Businessmen Blacks %	n	Whites %	n	Bay Ridge Merchants %	n	Total (All Samples) %	n
Automotive services	23	(13)	38	(8)	44	(9)	33	(30)
Other services	45	(40)	31	(19)	75	(4)	43	(63)
Low-cost items	33	(45)	37	(41)	16	(25)	31	(111)
High-cost items	33	(24)	22	(36)	33	(15)	28	(75)

this measure depends greatly on their type of business. Thus the whites score higher than the blacks in automotive services and low-cost items but the blacks score higher in Other Services and in high-cost items. This last finding is a further reminder of the disparity between relative success and absolute success, for it is in precisely the high-cost-item category that the whites far exceed the blacks in gross sales.

In the previous chapter we hypothesized that preparation for business, as measured by our index of business background, would lead to the reduction of business problems. The data on the blacks tended to support the hypothesis but for the Harlem whites the opposite relationship was found. Given the previous results, we might well be cautious about asserting a causal connection between business background and relative success. Nonetheless, it is of some interest to see whether a relationship exists between these characteristics. Table 5.13 presents the data.

Only among Bay Ridge merchants is there any hint that business background is associated with judgments of relative success. Among Harlem whites, those with a strong business background are more likely to view themselves as successful but the pattern is too irregular to provide much confidence in the result. Among blacks the figures are even more contradictory. Those with the strongest business background are least likely to judge themselves as successful. There is also no consistent difference between the blacks and whites of Harlem.

In Chapter 3 merchants were classified according to how carefully they kept records on their business activities. The assumption was that keeping good records was a sign of the good businessman. If this logic is correct we should find that record-keeping is related to the merchants' judgments of their progress; that is, their relative success. The validity of this argument can be assessed from Table 5.14.

From the columns of Table 5.14 we learn that record-keeping is *not* related to relative success. (The hint of such a relationship among the Bay Ridge merchants is suspect because there are so few merchants in the "good" category.) And from the rows, we find blacks who are fair or good on record-keeping are more likely than Harlem whites to score high on relative success. Only among those poor on record-keeping do the whites outscore the blacks.

We next examine the connection, if any, between *reported* problems and relative success. Do the merchants who admit to problems with suppliers, with sources of capital, and with insurance view their firms as less successful than those who do not perceive these problems? Table 5.15 shows this relationship.

The columns of Table 5.15 suggest that reported problems is negatively related to relative success. The pattern is clearest among the Harlem blacks, but it is also suggested by the data on the Harlem whites and Bay Ridge merchants. The merchant who is aware of problems and defines them as such is not as likely to be optimistic about his business. In two of the three rows the blacks are more likely than the whites to score high on success. (Among those scoring medium, the reverse is true.) But these differences are not large.

The pattern becomes much more irregular when we move from reported problems to "objective" problems, as can be seen from Table 5.16.

The columns of Table 5.16 do not show any relationship between objective problems and relative success, contrary to the negative relationship found for reported problems. This is not too surprising for we have already learned that these two indices of problems do not measure the same phenomenon. Thus reported problems was found to be positively related to size of store, but the objective problem index was found to be negatively related to size. The rows of Table 5.16 show a completely inconsistent pattern. Thus among those low on objective problems, there is little difference among the three samples; in the medium category both the blacks and Bay Ridge merchants do better than the Harlem whites, and among those high on objective problems, the Harlem whites come out better than the blacks.

TABLE 5.13

PERCENTAGE HIGH ON RELATIVE SUCCESS, BY BUSINESS BACKGROUND INDEX

Business Background	Harlem Merchants				Bay Ridge Merchants		Total (All Samples)	
	Blacks		Whites					
	%	n	%	n	%	n	%	n
Weak	33	(58)	36	(25)	17	(6)	33	(89)
Moderate	46	(41)	20	(55)	32	(28)	31	(124)
Strong	23	(22)	50	(24)	32	(19)	35	(65)

TABLE 5.14

PERCENTAGE HIGH ON RELATIVE SUCCESS, BY RECORD-KEEPING INDEX

Record-Keeping	Harlem Merchants				Bay Ridge Merchants		Total (All Samples)	
	Blacks		Whites					
	%	n	%	n	%	n	%	n
Poor	19	(21)	32	(19)	27	(11)	25	(51)
Fair	43	(73)	35	(68)	27	(37)	37	(178)
Good	30	(27)	12	(17)	60	(5)	27	(49)

TABLE 5.15

PERCENTAGE HIGH ON RELATIVE SUCCESS, BY REPORTED PROBLEMS INDEX

Reported Problems	Harlem Merchants				Bay Ridge Merchants		Total (All Samples)	
	Blacks		Whites					
	%	n	%	n	%	n	%	n
Low	49	(35)	39	(33)	48	(23)	45	(91)
Medium	32	(47)	40	(40)	16	(25)	31	(112)
High	30	(40)	10	(31)	20	(5)	21	(76)

In the previous section we found that number of years at current location was not related to gross sales. We suggested that this variable might well represent the expansion of a successful business rather than the newness of the business. This variable also fails to be related to relative success, as in each sample only irregular patterns emerge.

Since relative success measures the fortunes of the businessmen over the two-year period prior to the interview as well as during the interview year, it is possible that the riots that occurred in Harlem have some influence on the businessman's assessment of his success. Those who had their businesses damaged during the riots might well take a more pessimistic view of their fortunes than those who escaped damage. Table 5.17 indicates that there is merit to this hypothesis.

Riot damage is negatively related to judgments of success both among the blacks and the whites. It is not known whether this means that the damage contributed to business losses or that the owner whose store was damaged has become more pessimistic about his business. Both processes are probably at work. It should also be noted that there is no difference between the black and white merchants whose stores escaped damage, as about the same proportion of each group are in the highest category on relative success. But among those whose stores were damaged, a group that consists of more than twice as many whites as blacks, the white owners are less likely than the blacks to be high on relative success. The riot experience thus appears to have taken a greater toll on the whites than on the blacks, even among those who were affected.

The analysis in this section has shown that the blacks, in spite of their much lower gross sales, are somewhat more likely to be optimistic about the progress of their businesses than the Harlem whites. Thus they not only tend to score higher on relative success than the Harlem whites in general, but they do so even when size of firm is held constant. When type of firm is taken into account, the blacks again tend to hold their own, doing somewhat better than the whites in most types, but falling behind in automotive services. The possible impact on relative success of such variables as business experience, quality of record-keeping, reported problems, objective problems, years at current location, and riot experience were then examined. Although the scale occasionally tipped in favor of the Harlem whites, the blacks in general were more likely to score high on *relative* success when these variables were taken into account.

We turn in the next section to another indicator of "success," the businessman's commitment to remain in business at his current location.

Future Plans—Commitment to the Area

Having examined the correlates of gross sales, which have been treated as a crude indicator of absolute success, and the correlates of relative success, we turn now to more indirect indicators of the merchant's satisfaction with his business, those concerning his future plans. These include whether he plans to stay in business at the same location, move, or retire, and whether he is planning to sell his store.

Given the disturbances of the sixties, the growing consciousness of the black community, and the presumed increasing antagonisms toward whites in the black community, one might suppose that white merchants are likely to be making plans to leave Harlem. But the data on hand lend no suggestion to such an exodus in the making. When asked whether they were planning to stay at their current location, a substantial majority of both black and white Harlem merchants answered in the affirmative. Some were planning to go out of business because of ill health and retirement, and some did not know what they would do. The responses to this question for the Harlem merchants and the control group appear in Table 5.18.

About the same number of Harlem whites and blacks plan to stay at their present location. This pattern of continuity is

TABLE 5.16
PERCENTAGE HIGH ON RELATIVE SUCCESS, BY OBJECTIVE PROBLEM INDEX

| | Harlem Merchants | | | | Bay Ridge Merchants | | Total (All Samples) | |
| | Blacks | | Whites | | | | | |
Objective Problems	%	n	%	n	%	n	%	n
Low	29	(14)	31	(26)	26	(38)	28	(78)
Medium	49	(45)	27	(52)	55	(11)	39	(108)
High	29	(63)	39	(26)	—	(4)	30	(93)

TABLE 5.17
PERCENTAGE HIGH ON RELATIVE SUCCESS AMONG HARLEM BLACKS AND WHITES, BY RIOT EXPERIENCE

| | Harlem Merchants | | | |
| | Blacks | | Whites | |
Impact of the Riots	%	n	%	n
Store damaged	24	(17)	17	(36)
Store not damaged	39	(104)	38	(68)

TABLE 5.18
PLANS OF MERCHANTS (in percentages)

| | Harlem Merchants | | Bay Ridge Merchants |
Plans	Black	White	
Stay at current location	78	71	87
Move business	7	10	4
Retire or intend to go out of business	5	8	—
Do not know	10	10	9
Total	100	99	100
n	(122)	(105)	(53)

still stronger in the control group as 87 percent of the Bay Ridge merchants plan to remain at their present location. There is one respect, however, in which these data conceal a difference between black and white Harlem merchants. The 7 percent of the blacks who said they were planning to relocate represent 8 respondents, six of whom were planning to relocate within Harlem. In contrast, none of the 11 white merchants who plan to move intends to relocate in Harlem. The commitment to Harlem on the part of the black merchants is thus somewhat greater than Table 5.18 would suggest, but the important point is that a substantial majority of the white merchants in Harlem also plan to stay.

A somewhat different picture is provided by a related question. All the merchants were asked if they had any plans for selling their business. Some 20 percent of the Harlem whites answered affirmatively; another 12 percent were undecided; and 69 percent said they were not considering such a move. Among the blacks, only 8 percent were ready to sell their business; 9 percent were uncertain; and 83 percent were quite certain that they would not sell out. Again we find the Bay Ridge merchants behaving more like the Harlem blacks, as fully 85 percent were not interested in selling their business. These data indicate that a substantial minority of Harlem whites are at least considering the possibility of selling their business. To what extent is this related to plans for retirement, to lack of success, or to fear of the neighborhood?[7]

It is possible of course that the merchants who plan to sell their business or are uncertain about staying at their current location are the older men in our sample who are considering retirement. If so, we should find that the oldest merchants are least committed to maintaining their current business. Whether this is true can be seen from Table 5.19.

Hardly any Harlem merchants, black or white who are under 50, are not committed to staying where they are. Among blacks over 50, a somewhat smaller proportion are committed; and among whites over 50 there is a noticeable decline in this commitment. The pattern for the whites would suggest that the retirement thesis has merit, but even here the picture is ambiguous. Thus those whites least committed are not in the oldest age group but in the next to oldest, that is, men in their fifties, an age group that does not ordinarily consider retirement. Moreover, among the Bay Ridge merchants there is no support at all for the retirement thesis; the older and younger men are equally committed to remain in business.

Whether certainty about not selling is bolstered by success will be considered by showing its relationship to both gross sales and the index of relative success. Its connection with gross sales, our measure of absolute success, is shown in Table 5.20.

Among the Bay Ridge merchants gross sales has little to do with plans to stay in business. Among the blacks, those with gross sales under $25,000 are less certain than those with higher gross sales, but the most pronounced pattern is found among the Harlem whites. The table shows that a majority of the whites in the smallest gross sales category are either ready to sell out or are uncertain about selling, whereas this is true of only about one-quarter of the whites whose gross sales are higher. Thus "success" seems to be a definite factor in the decisions of the whites as to whether they will keep their business.

The role of success in commitment to keep the business is even more evident when the index of relative success is considered. As can be seen from Table 5.21, this relationship is quite strong for both the Harlem blacks and whites.

Again the commitment of the Bay Ridge merchants seems to be immune to success, for there is no relationship between the success index and commitment not to sell among the Bay Ridge merchants. But among the Harlem whites and blacks the relationship is strong. Only half the blacks who score low on success are certain of not selling their business, a figure that steadily increases to 91 percent of the blacks who score high on relative success. Among the whites, an even smaller

TABLE 5.19
PERCENTAGE DEFINITELY NOT
SELLING, BY AGE OF OWNER

| | Harlem Merchants | | | | Bay Ridge Merchants | |
| | Blacks | | Whites | | | |
Age of Owner	%	n	%	n	%	n
Under 40	90	(20)	88	(16)	88	(17)
40-49	85	(39)	96	(22)	86	(14)
50-59	77	(31)	50	(40)	92	(13)
60 and over	79	(29)	63	(24)	86	(7)

TABLE 5.20
PERCENTAGE DEFINITELY NOT
SELLING, BY GROSS SALES

| | Harlem Merchants | | | | Bay Ridge Merchants | |
| | Blacks | | Whites | | | |
Gross Sales	%	n	%	n	%	n
Under $25,000	76	(54)	41	(17)	88	(8)
$25,000-$99,999	93	(28)	73	(22)	100	(12)
$100,000 and over	87	(15)	75	(40)	85	(13)

TABLE 5.21
PERCENTAGE DEFINITELY NOT
SELLING, BY RELATIVE SUCCESS

| | Harlem Merchants | | | | Bay Ridge Merchants | |
| | Blacks | | Whites | | | |
Relative Success	%	n	%	n	%	n
Low	50	(16)	35	(17)	86	(7)
Medium low	84	(25)	63	(19)	100	(11)
Medium high	85	(34)	77	(35)	79	(19)
High	91	(43)	80	(30)	93	(14)

percentage of those in the low category, 35 percent, are committed to staying in business, and this increases to 80 percent of the whites in the high-success category. It should also be noted that on each level of success, proportionately more blacks than whites are committed to keeping their current business. This is true even among those who view their business as highly successful. These findings make clear that commitment is heavily dependent upon success, but the differences between blacks and whites suggest that other factors exist which affect commitment. Presumably, blacks are more ready than whites to stick it out regardless of their level of perceived success.

One further finding may be presented on the success theme as a factor in commitment. It will be recalled that one of the items that entered the index of relative success was how worried the merchant was that his business might fail. Those who were quite worried about failing should be less committed to staying in business, and Table 5.22 shows this to be so.

Hardly any Bay Ridge merchants worry about failure. But among the Harlem merchants, both black and white, worry about failure is clearly related to staying in business. The more worried these merchants are the less committed they are. This is especially true of those who were very worried about failing. As in the previous tables, we again find that the Harlem whites are less committed than the blacks to their current location. Thus on each level of worry, proportionately fewer of the whites are committed.

The lower commitment of the whites to remain at their current location, and presumably to remain in Harlem, might well be due in part to their perceiving the community as hostile or threatening. To test this possibility we shall consider the relationship of riot experience and having been the victim of a burglary or holdup to commitment.

The data confirm the fear hypothesis as a factor in the commitment of the whites. Thus among the blacks, there is little difference between those whose stores were damaged and those whose stores were not 80 percent compared with 83 percent. But among the whites, riot experience makes a significant difference in commitment not to sell as only 59 percent of those who suffered riot damage are prepared to stay compared with 73 percent of those whose stores were not damaged.

Still another indicator of the role that fear might play in the businessman's commitment to his current location is whether he has been held up or burglarized in the past two years. Table 5.23 shows that this experience does indeed affect commitment in each sample.

For the first time, we find the Bay Ridge businessmen behaving much as the Harlem merchants with respect to commitment. In every sample those who have been victims of larceny are less committed to remaining at their current location. This kind of experience seems to affect the commitment of the Harlem whites even more than that of the blacks or the Bay Ridge merchants. Thus the Harlem whites who were not victims of such crimes are only slightly less committed to staying where they are than are the blacks. But among the victims, the whites are much less committed than the blacks. A percentage difference in the former group of 8 points increases to one of 15 points in the latter group.

This analysis of commitment has shown that success is a key factor in the merchant's decision to remain in business. The more successful the merchant, whether measured by gross sales or by the index of relative success, the more likely he is to be committed to his current location. But even when success was taken into account, the Harlem blacks were more likely to be committed than the Harlem whites. Much of this difference was explained by the whites' greater fear of the community. Thus whites who had been victims of the riots and of crimes were much less committed than blacks who had similar experiences.

TABLE 5.22
PERCENTAGE DEFINITELY NOT SELLING, BY FEAR OF FAILURE

Worries About Failure	Harlem Merchants				Bay Ridge Merchants	
	Blacks		Whites			
	%	n	%	n	%	n
Very worried	47	(15)	40	(15)	67	(3)
Somewhat worried	89	(18)	63	(16)	88	(8)
Not at all worried	87	(85)	75	(67)	90	(40)

TABLE 5.23
PERCENTAGE DEFINITELY PLANNING TO REMAIN AT CURRENT LOCATION BY LARCENY EXPERIENCE

Larceny Experience	Harlem Merchants				Bay Ridge Merchants	
	Blacks		Whites			
	%	n	%	n	%	n
Burglarized and/or held up	76	(68)	61	(64)	79	(19)
Neither burglarized nor held up	90	(51)	82	(38)	93	(30)

Summary

We have looked at three facets of success: the merchants' gross sales, various indicators of relative success over time, and commitment to remain in business at the current location, the last being treated as an indirect measure of how successful the merchant has been. Harlem whites far exceed the blacks in gross sales, a finding that could not be explained by such factors as size of business, type of business, various indicators of business experience and talents, and problems confronting the business. It is not known whether the whites constitute a majority of the Harlem businessmen, for in this less than representative sample, they are a minority. But even if they are a minority, it is quite evident from the data on gross sales that in terms of dollar volume of business, they account for a substantial majority of the funds expended in the community.

When it came to relative success (that is, the businessman's judgment of how well he is doing relative to his past experience and his confidence that he will not fail), the blacks performed somewhat better than the whites, even though this index of relative success was related to gross sales on which the whites do better than the blacks. This seeming contradiction between the data on gross sales and relative success can be resolved by keeping in mind that the white-owned businesses of Harlem tend to be older than those owned by the blacks. The whites, as the earlier arrivals, might well see their businesses in a state of decline even though they may be making substantial profits and have greater gross sales. As the newcomers, the blacks might see themselves as making progress toward the goal of business success, even though they still have a long way to go to catch up with the whites.

The merchants' commitment to his current establishment was examined. Success proved to be a major factor, but for all merchants and in particular the Harlem whites, experi-

ences which generate fear were found to undermine commitment.

   This chapter concludes our analysis of the survey results.
The next and final chapter recapitulates the main findings
from the point of view of their implications for the Harlem
Commonwealth Council's proposed action program.

Chapter 6

SOME CONCLUSIONS AND RECOMMENDATIONS

We should like to call attention here to those findings that have implications for the goals of the Harlem Commonwealth Council—stimulating new black business and assisting blacks already in business in overcoming their problems.

Chapter 4 identified a number of the problems facing merchants in the Harlem community, particularly black merchants. It is clear that the black merchants have less efficient arrangements with suppliers, in part because they own smaller firms and cannot afford to buy merchandise in large lots. Even when size was taken into account, Harlem blacks were found to be more likely to deal with jobbers and more likely to pay C.O.D. for merchandise. The latter arrangement in particular is a hardship. That blacks have less credit than whites with their suppliers means that they cannot buy as many goods at any one time and that their capital reserves are necessarily smaller. Merchants buying on credit can use income from sales to pay for the merchandise, a privilege withheld from merchants required to pay C.O.D.

Clearly there is a great need for the black merchants to establish credit with suppliers and it is equally clear that they must have greater access to more economical suppliers. One of HCC's plans is to develop buying co-ops. We have seen that the black merchants are much more receptive to such an idea than whites and they obviously need the advantages that such co-ops can offer. HCC would do well to explore the feasibility of co-ops and work toward their creation. Under the current state of affairs, the Harlem blacks cannot compete effectively with the whites who have greater access to more economical arrangements for buying goods.

Black retailers need not only better arrangements with suppliers, but also more availability of business loans and investment capital. Blacks were less likely than whites to seek business loans, a finding related to the smaller size of their businesses, but significantly, those who did seek loans were more likely than the whites to have been turned down. HCC might well develop a program for increasing the opportunities for black businessmen to procure loans. This might be done through some educational program to encourage the existing lenders, namely the banks of the community, to change their policies about loans to black businessmen who cannot offer much security. Or HCC might pioneer in developing new institutions for making loans to black businessmen. It is conceivable that with the help of the government, new types of lending institutions can be created that would be sensitive to the needs of the black businessmen and would apply more flexible criteria for assessing risk.

The findings of Chapter 4 also confirmed that insurance is a critical problem for the ghetto merchant, black and white alike. Most striking here was the finding that a substantial minority of the black-owned businesses had no insurance protection. Thus, HCC might lobby for some plan of group insurance under which insurance companies would pool their resources and share the risks of providing insurance to ghetto merchants at reasonable rates.

Still another finding presented in Chapter 4 has clear

implications for HCC. We saw that black merchants, even more than the whites, complained about the difficulty of finding competent employees. It may well be that there are a number of jobs in Harlem retail establishments that remain vacant because of the paucity of trained personnel. Perhaps HCC can develop a training program for young blacks that would prepare them for the roles of clerk and salesman in small retail businesses.

In Chapter 3 we learned that blacks were less likely than whites to extend credit to customers. Just as they themselves are unable to get credit from suppliers, they in turn are less ready to give credit to their customers. And there may well be a causal connection here, for the blacks may simply not have the capital reserves to offer credit. If, as we assume, credit is a need of the consumers in Harlem, then HCC might well consider ways of increasing the capability and willingness of black merchants to extend credit. If the problem stems from the merchant's short supply of capital, then there is no ready solution. To the extent, however, that the blacks withhold credit from their customers out of fear of not being paid, then the black businessmen might well benefit from an educational program on credit management.

Perhaps the most significant finding in this entire report is the vast discrepancy in gross sales between black and white Harlem merchants. Whatever the number of black businessmen, it is evident that they control a much smaller share of dollar volume than the whites. How to narrow this gap is, of course, a difficult question. But it should be noted that the type of black-owned business with the largest gross sales is automotive services, consisting largely of gasoline stations. In this category blacks appear to compete successfully with whites. HCC has sought to develop several types of businesses in the automotive field, and on the basis of our findings these efforts would seem to have a pay-off.

Another finding deserving of study deals with the higher frequency of the preparation of financial reports among black merchants. We saw that this was especially prevalent among small retailers. Since record-keeping was not related to the success measures, the question must be raised as to the value of such frequent reports. We have conjectured that this practice stems from the salesmanship of firms that offer the service. If true, then HCC might well conduct an educational campaign on the types of records businessmen should keep and the best methods of their preparation.

Although the data were somewhat ambiguous, it appeared that Harlem blacks with a strong background in business had higher gross sales than those with a weak business background. Our measure of business background included having relatives in business and business experience, two matters that are not easily manipulatable. But it also included membership in trade associations, subscriptions to trade journals, and completion of courses in business. It may be suggested that in the long run the cause of black entrepreneurship will be furthered by interesting black youths in a business career and in preparing them through formal education. This education need not consist of enrollment at a school of business. Courses in the black community designed for those already in business and for those who may choose business as a career should yield a great pay-off. Some programs of this type have already been developed, particularly for those already in business. HCC might well concentrate on developing programs for youths who have not had the opportunity to consider the merits of a career in business.

Undoubtedly there are many other suggestions for action programs that stem from the findings of this report which the informed reader will discover for himself. Our primary task was to present in detail the situation of merchants in the Harlem community and to show ways in which the circumstances of black businessmen differed from those of the whites. Hopefully, we have enlarged the factual basis upon which a successful action program can be built.

APPENDIX: THE QUESTIONNAIRE

HARLEM BUSINESSMEN QUESTIONNAIRE

Time Begun _____
I.D. _____ 1-3

Structure of Business

1. What type of establishment is this?   4-7

2. Are you the sole owner of this store, is it owned by a partnership, or a corporation?   8-

Sole owner	(go to question 3)	1
Partnership	(go to part B)	2
Corporation		3

   A. Is it a closed or open corporation?   9-

Closed corporation	1
Open corporation	2

   B. What percentage of the business is yours?   10-11

_____ %

   C. Is (are) the other owner(s) relatives or members of your family?   12-

All are	1
Some are	2
None are	3

3. Did you start this business?   13-

       Yes   (go to question 4)   1
       No   2

  A. How did you get it?   14-

       Inherited it   1
       Purchased it   2
       Other (specify)_____

  B. Did you work here before you got it?   15-

       Yes   1
       No   2

4. How long have you owned the business at this address?   16-

       Less than 1 year   1
       1 to 2 years   2
       2 to 3 years   3
       3 to 5 years   4
       5 to 10 years   5
       10 or more years   6

5. Did you have this line of business at some other location
before you came here?   17-

       Yes   1
       No   (go to question 6)   2

  A. What attracted you to this particular location, was it . . .   18-

       Low rental?   1
       Knowledge of the neighborhood?   2
       Familiarity with customers?   3
       Busy street?   4
       No other business of this type nearby?   5
       Other (specify) _____

6. Is this the only store you own?   19-

       Yes   (go to question 7)   1
       No   2

  A. How many other stores do you own?   20-

                        # _____

B. Are the other stores the same kind of store as this one?   21-

        Same   1
        Other   2

7. Is this store owned on a franchise basis?   22-

        Yes   1
        No   2

8. Do you own this building, do you have a leaseback arrangement, or do you rent?   23-

        Own   (go to question 9)   1
        Leaseback   (go to question 9)   2
        Rent   3

A. How long a lease do you have?   24-

        Month to month   1
        Annual   2
        Two years   3
        Two years +   4
        Other (specify) _____

B. What is your monthly rent?   25-27

                  $_____

C. Are utilities (gas and electricity) included in your rent?   28-

        Yes   1
        No   2

D. Is your rental a flat rate or a percentage of gross sales or combination of both?   29-

        Flat rate   (go to question 9)   1
        % of gross   2
        Combination   3

E. What is the percentage of gross sales?   30-31

            _____%

9. What is the total square footage (including basement, etc.) that you have here?   32-36

            _____ sq. ft.

10. Do you maintain storage space elsewhere?   37-

        Yes   1
        No   2

11. How many days per week are you open?   38-

_____

A. When do you open the store and when do you close?

Monday	Open ____	Close ____	Total ____
Tuesday	____	____	____
Wednesday	____	____	____
Thursday	____	____	____
Friday	____	____	____
Saturday	____	____	____
Sunday	____	____	____

39-40

Total Number of Hours_____

Personnel

12. Some businessmen in this area seem to have a problem finding competent help. Do you have this problem?   41-

Yes   1
No   (go to question 13)   2

A. Please explain.   42-43

13. Including yourself, how many people work here?   44-45

_____

If Only One Person, Go To Question 22

If Other Persons Besides Respondent—Ask:

14. Are any of these members of your family?   46-

Yes   1
No   (go to question 15)   2

A. How many members of your family work here?   47-

_____

B. How many hours per week do these family members work in the store (all together)?   48-49

_____ hrs.

C. Do these family members receive a regular salary?   50-

Yes, all   (go to question 21)   1
Yes, some   (go to question 21)   2
No, none   (go to question 22)   3

If there are Non-Family Employees in Addition to the Family – Ask:

15. How many of your non-family employees are full time?   51-

\# _____

16. How many are part time?   52-

\# _____

17. What is the racial composition of your non-family employees?
(Find out Number in Each Category)

Negroes   \# _____   53-
Spanish-speaking   \# _____   54-
Other   \# _____   55-

18. Apart from sales help, do you have any office personnel?   56-

Yes   1
No   (go to question 19)   2

A. How many?   57-

\# _____

19. Aside from sales help, do you have any security personnel?   58-

Yes   1
No   (go to question 20)   2

A. How many?   59-

\# _____

20. Approximately how many of your employees live in
Harlem?   60-

\# _____

21. What is your gross *weekly* payroll?   61-65

(go to question 22) $ _____
Don't know _____ 66-1

A. (*If Don't Know – Ask*) What is your gross annual
payroll?   67-72

$ _____

Customers

22. Do most of your customers live in Harlem or do they come from outside?   4-

        Harlem   1
        Outside Harlem   2

23. About what percentage of your customers would you say are Negroes?   5-6

_____ %

24. About what percentage are white?   7-8

_____ %

25. About what percentage are Spanish-speaking?   9-10

_____ %

26. About what percentage of your customers are repeat customers?   11-12

_____ %

27. About what percentage of your customers do you know by name?   13-14

_____ %

28. About what percentage of your customers are on welfare? 15-16

_____ %

29. About how many customers do you have on a typical day?   17-19

_____

30. In the past couple of years has there been a change in the kind of customers you have?   20-

        Yes   1
        No   (go to question 31)   2
        Doesn't apply   9

  A. How have they changed?   21-22

Credit Customers

31. Do you extend credit to your customers?   23-

        Yes   (go to question 32)   1
        No   2

A. Have you ever extended credit to customers?   24-

        Yes   1
        No   (go to question 38)   2

B. Why did you stop extending credit?   25-26

32. What percentage of your total sales is credit sales?   27-28

        ————————————————— %

33. What type of credit do you extend?   29-

        Book Credit ONLY   (go to question 37)   1
        Credit Card ONLY   (go to question 38)   2
        Revolving Credit ONLY   (go to question
        37)   3
        Revolving & Credit Card   (go to
        question 37)   4
        Installment Credit ONLY   5
        Installment & Credit Card   6
        Installment & Revolving   7
        Installment, Revolving & Credit Card   8

34. Do you make your credit customers fill out a credit
application?   30-

        Yes   1
        No   (go to question 35)   2

A. Do you check this information?   31-

        Yes   1
        No   2

35. When extending credit, do you make your customers sign
an installment contract?   32-

        Yes   1
        No   (go to question 37)   2

36. Do you keep all of your installment contracts, do you sell
some of them or do you sell all of them?   33-

        Keep all   (go to question 37)   1
        Sell some   2
        Sell all   3

    A. What are your reasons for selling these contracts?   34-35

37. What is the percentage of loss on your credit accounts?   36-37

                                 _____ %

    A. How do you calculate this?   38-39

    B. In the past two years has your loss rate been increasing, decreasing or remaining the same?   40-

Increasing	1
Decreasing	2
Remaining the same	3

38. Do you make use of a lay-away plan?   41-

Yes	1
No	2

39. Do you maintain your prices or do your customers bargain with you?   42-

Maintain prices	1
Bargain	2

Advertising and Promotion

40. Do you spend money on advertising?   43-

Yes	1
No (go to question 41)	2

    A. What method of advertising do you use?   44-

Window announcements?	1
Newspapers?	2
Mail Circulars?	3
Radio?	4
Other (specify) _____	45-

41. Do you ever have sales?   46-

Yes	1
No (go to question 42)	2

A. How often do you have these sales?   47-

Continually	1
Weekly	2
Monthly	3
Seasonally	4
Annually	5
Semi-annually	6

B. What kinds of sales do you have?   48-

General markdown	1
Special markdown	2
Loss leaders	3
Clearance	4
Other (specify) _____	

C. What are your reasons for having sales?   49-50

(Interviewer: Check Whether Store has a Window Display)   51-

Display	1
No display	2

42. How often do you change window displays?   52-

Weekly	1
Monthly	2
Seasonally	3
Semi-annually	4
Annually	5
No displays	6

43. Have you found window displays helpful for your business?   53-

Yes (go to question 44)	1
No	2

A. Why aren't they helpful?   54-55

Record-Keeping

44. (*Ask if in Doubt*) Do you have a cash register?   56-

Yes (go to part D)	1
No	2

A. Do you use an adding machine instead of a cash register?   57-

Yes	1
No	2

B. Have you ever had a cash register?   58-

Yes	1
No (go to question 45)	2

C. What happened to it?   59-60

D. Does the cash register have a tape?   61-

Yes	1
No (go to question 45)	2

E. Do you bother to check the tape daily?   62-

Yes	1
No	2

45. Do you keep sales slips?   63-

Yes	1
No (go to question 46)	2

A. Do you bother to check the sales slips against the tape?   64-

Yes	1
No	2
Sometimes	3

46. Can you tell how your sales at this time of year compare with your sales at the same time last year?   65-

Yes	1
No	2

47. Do you usually make such comparisons?   66-

Yes	1
No	2

48. Do you keep a systematic record of all the money that you take in and all the money you spend in the business?   67-

Yes	1
No	2

49. How often do you have a financial statement preparef for your business? 68-

Monthly	1
Quarterly	2
Semi-annually	3
Annually	4

   A. Who prepares the statement? 69-

Self (go to question 50)	1
Someone else	2

   B. Who does it? _____ 70-
                                (Give occupational title)

50. Generally, what do you learn from these financial statements?
                                                 71-72

51. How important are these statements for you in running your business? 73-

Very important	1
Fairly important	2
Not too important	3

52. Do you prepare your tax returns yourself or does someone else prepare it for you? 74-

Self (go to question 53)	1
Someone else	2

   A. Who prepares it? _____ 75-
                              (Give occupational title)   79-80
                                                   02

53. Do you have any system for keeping track of what you have in stock? 4-

Yes	1
No (go to part B)	2

   A. Do you keep a perpetual inventory? 5-

Yes (go to question 54)	1
No	2

B. Do you take physical inventory (go through the store and count what you have)?   6-

Yes   (go to question 54)   1
No   2

C. How do you know when to order merchandise?   7-

D. How do you determine inventory for tax purposes?   8-

54. How many times per year do you estimate that your inventory turns over?   9-

\# _____

Suppliers

55. Many Harlem merchants complain about problems with suppliers. Do you have problems?   10-

Yes   1
No   (go to question 56)   2

A. What kinds of problems?   11-12

56. Are there lines of merchandise that you would like to have but suppliers won't let you have?   13-

Yes   1
No   (go to question 57)   2

A. What is (are) the line(s) of merchandise that they will not supply?   14-16

_____

_____

_____

B. Who are these suppliers?   17-19

    C. Why won't they give you these lines?   20-21

57. Do you get your merchandise or supplies from: 22-

        Manufacturers?   1
        Wholesalers?   2
        Jobbers?   3

58. Generally, do you pay your suppliers: 23-

        C.O.D.?   1
        2/10 net 30?   2
        Within 30 days?   3
        Within 60 days?   4
        Other (specify) _____

59. Do you have trouble in obtaining credit from suppliers?   24-

        Yes   1
        No   (go to question 60)   2

  A. Why is that?   25-26

60. Are you behind in your payments to suppliers?   27-

        Yes   1
        No (go to question 61)   2

  A. Are you worried that you will be unable to make these
payments?   28-

        Yes   1
        No   2

61. What actions do suppliers usually take when you are behind
on payments?   29-30

62. Do you always buy from the same suppliers?   31-

        Yes (go to question 63)   1
        No   2

  A. Why don't you?   32-33

63. What do you think of the idea of forming "buying cooperatives?"   34-

Good idea	1
Bad idea	2
Don't understand	3

64. Would you personally be interested in purchasing your
merchandise or supplies by pooling orders with other merchants?   35-

Yes	1
No	2

Capital and Credit

65. Some merchants seem to have problems getting capital for
their business. Is this a major problem for you or not much of
a problem?   36-

Major problem	1
Not much of a problem	2

66. Where did you obtain the capital to start in this business?   37-

Savings (go to question 67)	1
Relatives or Friends (go to question 67)	2
Loans	3
Other (specify) (go to question 67)	

_____

A. Where did you get the loan?   38-

Bank	1
Finance Company	2
Small Business Admin.	3
Other (specify) _____	

B. For how many years was the loan made?   39-40

_____

C. Are you still paying on that loan?   41-

Yes	1
No	2

67. Have you ever borrowed money for business purposes?   42-

Yes (go to question 68)	1
No	2

A. Is that because you don't need to borrow or because you have difficulty getting loans?   43-

Don't need (go to question 73)	1
Have difficulty (go to question 71)	2

68. When was the last time that you borrowed money for business?   44-

1968	1
1967	2
1966	3
1965	4
Before 1965 (specify)_____	

69. Where did you borrow the money?   45-

Bank	1
Finance Company (Ask A)	2
Small Business Administration	3
Friends or Relatives (Ask A)	4
Other (specify) _____	

A. Why did you borrow from them instead of a bank?   46-47

70. What was the true annual interest rate on this loan?   48-49

_____ %

Don't know   99

71. Have you ever been turned down for a loan by a financial institution?   50-

Yes	1
No (go to question 73)	2

A. Why were you turned down?   51-52

B. Who turned you down?   53-

Bank	1
Finance Company	2
Small Business Administration (go to question 73)	3
Other (specify) _____	

72. Have you ever tried to borrow money from the Small Business
Administration?   54-

        Yes   1
        No   (Ask A)   2

  A. Why haven't you ever tried to borrow from them?   55-56

  B. Did you succeed in obtaining the loan?   57-

        Yes   (go to question 73)   1
        No   2
  C. Why not?   58-59

73. Suppose you needed money for your business today, where
would you go for a loan?   60-

        Bank   1
        Finance Company   2
        Small Business Administration   3
        Friends or Relatives   4
        Other (specify) _____

74. Have you ever borrowed from a lender who charged
extremely high interest rates?   61-

        Yes   1
        No   2

75. Would you now borrow from such a lender as a last resort?   62-

        Yes   1
        No   2
        Depends   3

Competitors

76. Where is your chief competitor located?   63-

        Same block   1
        One block away   2
        More than one block   3
        Don't know   (go to question 79)   4

77. Does he carry a bigger or smaller line of merchandise than you do?   64-

Bigger	1
Smaller	2
Same	3
Don't know	4

78. Are his prices higher, lower, or about the same as yours?   65-

Higher	1
Lower	2
Same	3
Don't know	4

79. Are you often forced to lower your prices because of competition?   66-

Yes	1
No	2

80. Within the past year have you lost business because of competition?   67-

Yes	1
No	2

Insurance and Police Protection

81. Another problem that many Harlem merchants have is getting insurance for their business. What kinds of insurance do you now carry?   68-

Fire (go to question 82)	1
Theft (go to question 82)	2
Plate Glass (go to question 82)	3
Riot (go to question 82)	4
Liability (go to question 82)	5
None	6

A. Why don't you now carry insurance?   69-70

B. Have you ever carried insurance?   71-

Yes	1
No (go to question 86)	2

82. Have you ever had any insurance policies cancelled?   72-

        Yes   1
        No   (go to question 83)   2

  A. Which ones?   73-

        Fire   1
        Theft   2
        Plate Glass   3
        Riot   4
        Liability   5
        None   (go to question 83)   6

  B. Why was (were) the policy (policies) cancelled?   74-75

                                                          79-80
                                                         0-3

83. What kind(s) of insurance do you now have trouble getting?   4-

        Fire   1
        Theft   2
        Plate Glass   3
        Riot   4
        Liability   5
        None   6

84. About how much per year does all your insurance cost?   5-8

                            $ _____

85. Has the cost of your insurance gone up during the past few
years?   9-

        Yes   1
        No   2

  A. About what percentage has it gone up?   10-11

                         _____ %

86. Was your store damaged during the racial disturbances in
the past couple of years in this area?   12-

        Yes   1
        No   (go to question 87)   2

  A. During which years?   13-14

B. How extensive was the damage?   15-

87. Are you worried about this happening to your store in the
future?   16-

Yes	1
No	2

88. Is shoplifting a major problem in your business?   17-

Yes	1
No	2

89. Do you have any problems with employees stealing cash or
merchandise?   18-

Yes	1
No	2

90. How many times during the past two years has this store
been burglarized?   19-

                                    # _____

91. How many times during the last two years have you been
held up?   20-

                                    # _____

92. Do you think the police do a good job of protecting your
store?   21-

Yes	1
No	2

93. How would you describe your relations with the police?
Would you say they are very good, fairly good or not too good? 22-

Very good	1
Fairly good	2
Not too good	3

Neighborhood

94. Do you think that this area has improved or deteriorated
during the last year?   23-

Improved (go to question 95)	1
Deteriorated	2
Remained the same (go to question 95)	3

A. How has it deteriorated?   24-25

B. Has the decline in the area affected your business?   26-

                    Yes   1
                    No   2

95. Have the merchants around here tried to improve the area? 27-

                    Yes   1
                    No   (go to question 96)   2

A. What have they done?   28-29

B. Have you participated in these efforts?   30-

                    Yes   1
                    No   2

96. Are you planning to stay at this location or are you planning
to leave?   31-

                    Plan to stay   (go to question 97)   1
                    Plan to move   2
                    Going out of business (go to part B)   3
                    Don't know   (go to question 97)   4

A. Where would you relocate?   32-

                    In Harlem   1
                    Manhattan outside Harlem   2
                    Bronx   3
                    Brooklyn   4
                    Queens   5
                    Long Island   6
                    Outside NYC   7

B. What are your reasons for moving (or going out of
business?   33-34

Profits and Volume of Business

97. Now I would like to ask you a few questions about your business. How did your business do in 1967? Did you make money, did you break even or did you lose money?   35-

Made money (go to question 98)	1
Broke Even (go to question 98)	2
Lost money (go to question 98)	3
Not in business in 1967	4

A. How is your business doing? Are you making money, breaking even or losing money?   36-

Making money (go to question 100)	1
Breaking even (go to question 100)	2
Losing money (go to question 100)	3

98. Did you do better in 1967 than in 1966, about the same or worse?   37-

Better in 1967	1
About the same in 1967	2
Worse in 1967	3

99. How about this year, do you think you will do better, about the same or worse than last year?   38-

Better this year	1
About the same this year	2
Worse this year	3

100. In the past year, did you do any of the following?   39-

Increase personnel	1
Increase inventory	2
Sell more lines	3
Modernize store	4
Enlarge store	5

101. Have you any plans for selling this business?   40-

Yes	1
No (go to question 102)	2
Don't know (go to question 102)	3

A. What are your reasons for wanting to sell?   41-42

B. Do you have any prospective buyers?   43-

        Yes   (go to part D)   1
        No   2

C. Are you actively looking for buyers?   44-

        Yes   1
        No   2

D. Roughly, when do you think that you will get out of
business here?   45-46

E. If you do sell out, will you be continuing in business elsewhere, will you be going into different work or will you retire?   47-

        Business elsewhere   1
        Going into different work   2
        Retiring   3

102. What do you think is the good-will value or key value of
your store?   48-51

103. What do you estimate the selling price of your business
to be?   52-57

                            $ _____

104. How worried are you that your business might fail?
Would you say you are . . .   58-

        Very worried   1
        Somewhat worried   2
        Not too worried   (go to question 105)   3

A. Why is that?   59-60

If this is a New Business—Go to Question 106

105. Would you look at this card and tell me into which
category your gross sales for the last year fell? *(Show Card and
Record Category)*   61-

106. Into which category would you anticipate your gross sales for this year will fall? *(Show Card and Record Category)*   62-

_____

Business Background

Just a few questions about your business background and we're finished.

107. In all, how many years have you been in business for yourself?   63-64

_____

108. Before you started this business, did you own any other business or were you working for someone else?   65-

                  Owned other business   (go to question 109) 1
                  Worked for someone else   2
                  Other (specify)_____
                    (go to question 109)

    A. In what capacity did you work?   66-67

_____

109. Why did you go into business?   68-69

110. How old were you when you first seriously considered business as a career?   70-71

_____

111. Were any of your close relatives ever in business?   72-

                  Yes   1
                  No   2

112. Have you ever taken any courses to prepare yourself for business?   73-

                  Yes   1
                  No   (go to question 113)   2

    A. What courses did you take?   74-75

                                        76-77
                                        78-79
                                        79-80
                                        0-4

113. Do you belong to any trade associations?   4-

        Yes   1
        No   2

114. Do you subscribe to or read regularly any trade or business publications?   5-

        Yes   1
        No   (go to question 115)   2

  A. Which ones?   6-7

                                                       8-9
                                                     10-11

115. Where were you born?   12-13

If Born Outside New York City—Ask:

  A. How many years have you lived in this area?   14-15

                                      _____yrs.

116. How old are you?   16-

20-24	1	45-49	6
25-29	2	50-54	7
30-34	3	55-59	8
35-39	4	60 and over	9
40-44	5	No answer	0

117. When you were in school, what was your father's occupation?   17-18

118. What was the highest grade you completed in school?   19-

        Grammar School or less   1
        Some High School   2
        High School Graduate   3
        Some College   4
        College Graduate   5
        No Answer   6

119. Are you . . .   20-

Married   1
Divorced   (go to part B)   2
Widowed   (go to part B)   3
Separated   (go to part B)   4
Single   (go to question 121)   5

A. Does your wife (husband) have a regular job?   21-

No   1
Yes, full time   2
Yes, part time   3

B. Do you have any children?   22-

Yes   1
No   (go to question 121)   2

C. How would you feel about your children going into
business?   23-

Approve   1
Disapprove   2
Don't Care   3

121. Where do you live?   24-

Harlem   1
Manhattan outside Harlem   2
Bronx   3
Brooklyn   4
Long Island   5
Queens   6
Outside NYC   7

122. Do you belong to any community organizations in Harlem? 25-

Yes   1
No   2

123. Oh! By the way, many businessmen in Harlem have been
complaining about the rising cost of police protection. Have your
costs risen or remained the same?   26-

Risen   1
Remained the same   2
Not paying for protection   3

124. How about other private protection costs? Have they risen or remained the same?   27-

Risen	1
Remained the same	2
Not paying for protection	3

To be Filled in by Interviewer

1. Time Ended _____   31-32

2. Elapsed time _____

3. Date of interview _____   33-35

4. Ethnicity of person interviewed: 36-

Black	1
White	2
Other	3
Don't know	9

5. Merchant's cooperation: 37-

Very cooperative	1
Somewhat cooperative	2
Uncooperative	3
Hostile	4

6. Location of store: 38-

Mid-block	1
Corner	2

7. Level of store: 39-

Basement	1
Street floor	2
2nd floor	3

8. In your opinion, does this store seem to be . . .   40-

Black-owned	1
Spanish-speaking-owned	2
White-owned	3
Other	4
Don't know	9

Observational Ratings by Interviewer

(Circle the Number which Represents your Estimate of Store's Rating)

9.	Store Cleanliness	Clean Floor Swept	1	2	3	4	5		Dirty Unswept	41-
10.	Stock Layout	Well Organized	1	2	3	4	5		Crowded Cluttered	42-
11.	Interior Lighting	Well Lit	1	2	3	4	5		Not well Lit	43-
12.	Paint	Freshly Painted	1	2	3	4	5		Needs Painting	44-
13.	Window Display	Appealing	1	2	3	4	5		Unappealing	45-
14.	Courtesy to Customers	Cordial	1	2	3	4	5		Ignored	46-
15.	Stock on Hand	Well Supplied	1	2	3	4	5		Scarcely Any	47-
16.	Store Front	Modern	1	2	3	4	5		Rundown	48-
17.	Air Conditioning	Yes	1				5		No	49-
18.	Store Front Gate	Yes	1				5		No	50-

19. Interviewer's Comments (*Anything that Seems to be Relevant*):   51-60

20. Name of Interviewer _____ 61-62

NOTES

1. Some 46 percent of our sample consists of whites. If they were replaced by blacks, 59 percent of whom lived in the community, the increase in local owners would come to 27 percent. If the proportions of black owners of different-sized firms living in Harlem were taken into account (Table 2.6), the increase would be less than 27 percent.

2. These averages were computed from grouped data and are based on the mid-points for the categories. The lowest category was under 70 hours, which we estimated as 55 on the average.

3. Thirteen of the black businessmen either were not asked or did not reply to the question about sales. Presumably, these merchants owned businesses which did not lend themselves to sales; e.g., eating and drinking establishments or funeral parlors.

4. One implication of the C.O.D. arrangement is that the merchant generally cannot afford to order in bulk and still pay cash. The advantage of the other arrangements is that he can sell part or all of the supplies *before* he has to pay for them. In this sense, the blacks who have to pay at time of delivery, are particularly disadvantaged relative to their white counterparts.

5. These percentages are smaller than those reported for the first question, indicating that some merchants in each group approve of buying cooperatives in principle even though they personally have no need for them.

6. It should be noted that the whites in Harlem were more reluctant than the blacks to answer this question—23 percent compared with 15 percent—and the true rates of refusals may be higher.

7. This question is somewhat ambiguous for it is not certain whether the man who plans to sell intends to leave retailing entirely or is only eager to leave the area and start a business in a different location. We assume that the question measures commitment to current location as well as to business in general.

REFERENCES

CAPLOVITZ, D. (1963) *The Poor Pay More*. New York: Free Press.

CHINOY, E. (1952) "Aspirations of automobile workers." Amer. J. of Sociology 57: 453-457.

GANS, H. J. (1969) "Negro-Jewish conflict in New York City: a sociological evaluation." Midstream (March): 3-15.

KOOS, E. L. (1946) *Families in Trouble*. New York: Kings Crown Press.

BIBLIOGRAPHY

MONOGRAPHS

Allen, Robert L., *Black Awakening in Capitalist America: An Analytic History,* Garden City, N.Y., Doubleday, 1969.

Andreasen, Alan R., *Inner City Business; a Case Study of Buffalo, N.Y.,* New York, Praeger, 1971.

Bailey, Ronald W., *Black Business Enterprise; Historical and Contemporary Perspectives,* New York, Basic Books, 1971.

Barry, Fred, et al., *A Study of Commercial Structure in Economically Depressed Neighborhoods,* Department of Marketing, Case Western Reserve University, 1968.

Bauer, Raymond A. and Scott M. Cunningham, *Studies in the Negro Market,* Cambridge, Mass., Marketing Science Institute, 1970.

Bell, Carolyn, *The Economics of the Ghetto,* New York, Pegasus, 1970.

Berkner, George E., "Black Capitalism and the Urban Negro," Tempe, Arizona, Bureau of Business and Economic Research, Occasional Paper No. 8, Arizona State University, 1970.

Berry, Brian J.L., et al., *The Impact of Urban Renewal on Small Business: The Hyde Park-Kenwood Case,* Chicago, Center for Urban Studies, The University of Chicago, 1968.

Brown, James K. and Seymour Lusterman, *Business and the Development of Ghetto Enterprise,* New York, Conference Board, 1971.

Burton, Robert C., et al., *Urban Small Business—An Analysis of Current Problems,* Richmond, Virginia Employment Commission, 1970.

Business in the Ghetto, The Business Lawyer, Vol. 25, September 1969 (Special issue).

Chicago Economic Development Corporation, *Retail Location Analysis Manual and Retailing in Low-Income Areas,* Chicago, CEDC, 1971.

Clark, Kenneth B., *Dark Ghetto: Dilemmas of Social Power,* New York, Harper and Row, 1965.

Coles, Flournoy A., Jr., *An Analysis of Entrepreneurship in Seven Urban Areas,* Washington, D.C., The National Business League, 1969.

Cross, Theodore L., *Black Capitalism: Strategy for Business in the Ghetto,* New York, Atheneum, 1969.

Davis, Frank G., *The Economics of Black Community Development: An Analysis and Program for Autonomous Growth and Development,* Chicago, Markham Publishing Co., 1972.

Drake, St. Clair, and Horace R. Cayton, *Black Metropolis,* New York, Harcourt Brace and Co., 1943.

Drexel Institute of Technology, *An Analysis of Little Business and the Little Businessman of Philadelphia,* Vols. I and II, Philadelphia, 1964.

--, *A Further Analysis of Little Business and the Businessman in Philadelphia,* Philadelphia, 1965.

DuBois, William E.B., *The Negro in Business,* New York, AMS Press, 1971, reprint of the 1899 edition.

Durham, Laird, *Black Capitalism: Critical Issues in Urban Management,* Washington, D.C. Published and distributed by Communication Service Corp. for Arthur D. Little, Inc., 1970.

Economic Development Opportunity, U.S. Senate, 90th Congress, "Role of the Federal Government in the Development of Small Business Enterprise in the Urban Ghetto." Hearings Before the Select Committee on Small Business, May 24, 1968, and June 17, 1968, Washington, D.C., U.S. Government Printing Office, 1968.

Economic Report on Installment Credit and Retail Sales Practices of District of Columbia Retailers, Bureau of Economics, Federal Trade Commission, March, 1968.

Epstein, Edwin M. and David R. Hampton, *Black Americans and White Business,* Encino, California, Dickenson Publishing Co., 1971.

Foley, Eugene P., *The Achieving Ghetto,* Washington, D.C., The Nation Press, 1968.

Forrester, Jay W., *Urban Dynamics,* Cambridge, Mass., MIT Press, 1969.

Ghetto Marketing: What Now? Proceedings of the American Marketing Association, Chicago, Illinois, Fall, 1968.

Gibson, D. Parke, *The $30 Billion Negro,* New York, Macmillan, 1969.

Ginzberg, Eli (ed.), *Business Leadership and the Negro Crisis,* New York, McGraw-Hill, 1968.

--(ed.), *The Negro Challenge to the Business Community,* New York, McGraw-Hill, 1964.

Gloster, Jesse E., *Minority Business Enterprise in Houston, Texas,* Houston, Department of Economics, Texas Southern University, 1969.

Haddad, William F. and G. Douglas Pugh (eds.), *Black Economic Development,* Englewood Cliffs, N.J., Prentice-Hall, 1969.

Harmon, John Henry, Arnett G. Lindsay and Carter G. Woodson, *The Negro as a Business Man*, College Park, Md., Mcgrath, 1969 c. 1929.

Harris, Abram L., *The Negro as Capitalist: A Study of Banking and Business Among American Negroes*, Philadelphia, American Academy of Political and Social Science, 1936.

Henderson, William L. and Larry C. Ledebur, *Economic Disparity — Problems and Strategies for Black America*, New York, The Free Press, 1970.

Holloway, Robert J. and Richard N. Cardozo, *Consumer Problems and Marketing Patterns in Low-Income Neighborhoods*, Graduate School of Business Administration, University of Minnesota, Minneapolis, 1969.

Hund, James M., *Black Entrepreneurship*, Belmont, Calif., Wadsworth, 1970.

Jones, Edward H., *Blacks in Business*, New York, Grosset & Dunlap, 1971.

Kain, John F. (ed.), *Race and Poverty: The Economics of Discrimination*, Englewood Cliffs, N.J., Prentice-Hall, 1969.

Kinzer, Robert H. and Edward Sagarin, *The Negro in American Business: Conflict Between Separatism and Integration*, New York, Greenberg, 1950.

Levitan, Sar A., *Federal Aid to Depressed Areas*, Baltimore, Johns Hopkins, 1964.

——, Garth L. Mangum and Robert Taggart III, *Economic Opportunity in the Ghetto: the Partnership of Government and Business* (Policy Studies in Employment and Welfare No. 3), Baltimore, The Johns Hopkins Press, 1970.

Light, Ivan Hubert, *Ethnic Enterprise in America: Business and Welfare Among Chinese, Japanese and Blacks*, Berkeley, University of California Press, 1972.

Little, Robert, *Alternative Ownership Forms for Inner City Businesses*, Graduate School of Business Administration, University of Washington, Seattle.

McCord, William, et al., *Life Styles in the Black Ghetto*, New York, W.W. Norton, 1969.

MacDonald, Stephen (comp.), *Business and Blacks; Minorities as Employees and Entrepreneurs*, Princeton, N.J., Dow Jones Books, 1970.

McLaurin, Dunbar S., *Ghediplan: Ghetto Economic Development and Industrialization Plan*, New York, Human Resources Administration, 1968.

Minority Enterprise, Journal of Small Business, Vol. 7, April-July 1969 (Special issue).

Morin, Bernard A. (ed.), *Marketing in a Changing World*, Chicago, American Marketing Association, 1969.

Northrup, Herbert R. and Richard L. Lowan, eds., *The Negro and Employment Opportunities*, Ann Arbor, University of Michigan, 1965.

Ofari, Earl, *The Myth of Black Capitalism*, New York, Monthly Review Press, 1970.

Plan of Action for Challenging Times, Inc., *Analysis of the Problems Encountered by the Neighborhood Grocery Cooperative in the Hunters Point-Bayview Region of San Francisco*, by Jean Boubee, San Francisco, California, PACT, Inc., 1969.

Pierce, Joseph Alphonso, *Negro Business and Business Education*, Westport, Conn., Negro Universities Press, 1971, c. 1947.

Proceedings of the National Black Economic Development Conference, Detroit, April 25-27, 1969.

Raine, Walter J., *Los Angeles Riot Study—The Ghetto Merchant Study*, Institute of Government and Public Affairs, MR-98, June 1, 1967.

Retailing in Low Income Areas, Real Estate Research Corporation, Chicago Small Business Opportunities Corporation, August, 1967.

Reubens, Edwin P., *Economic Strategies for the Ghetto*, City Almanac, Vol. 4, April 1970, New York, Center for New York City Affairs, New School for Social Research.

Rosenbloom, Bert, "Characteristics of Retailing in a Slum," Rider College, Trenton, N.J., 1971 (mimeographed).

Schuster, Louis H., *Business Enterprises of Negroes in Tennessee*, Washington, D.C., SBA, 1961.

Seder, John and Berkeley A. Burrell, *Getting It Together; Black Businessmen in America*, New York, Harcourt Brace Jovanovich, 1971.

Strang, William A., et al., *Consulting for Black Enterprise . . . A Challenge to the Business Establishment*, Milwaukee, The Center for Venture Management, 1970.

——, *Consulting for Black Enterprise . . . Experiences During the Second Year*, Milwaukee, The Center for Venture Management, 1971.

Sturdivant, Frederick D., *Business and Mexican American Relations in East Los Angeles*, Graduate School of Business Administration, University of Southern California, August 4, 1967.

——(ed.), *The Ghetto Marketplace*, New York, Free Press, 1969.

Tobb, William K., *The Political Economy of the Black Ghetto*, New York, W.W. Norton, 1970.

Vietorisz, Thomas and Bennett Harrison, *The Economic Development of Harlem*, New York, Praeger, 1970.

Washington, Booker T., *The Negro in Business*, New York, AMS Press, 1971, reprint of 1907 edition.

Weaver, Robert C., *The Negro Ghetto*, New York, Harcourt, Brace, 1948.

Wellisz, Stanislaw, "The Economy of Harlem," Department of Commerce Clearinghouse for Federal Scientific and Technical Information, Springfield, Virginia, 1969.

Wickstrom, David and John Holdridge, *Black Business in Minneapolis and St. Paul: A Comparative Study of Black and White Owned Businesses,* Minneapolis, Minn., 1971, 40 p.

ARTICLES

"Aiding Black Capitalism," Business Week, August 17, 1968, p. 32.

Alexander, Don H., "The Black Businessmen—Hope for the Future," University of Washington Business Review, Vol. 30, Winter 1971, pp. 15-20.

——, "What Do You Want, Mr. Black Businessman?" Economic Leaflets (Florida University), Vol. 30, January 1971, pp. 1-4.

Allen, Louis L., "Making Capitalism Work in the Ghettos," Harvard Business Review, Vol. 47, May-June 1969, pp. 83-92.

Allvine, Fred C., "Black Business Development," Journal of Marketing, Vol. 34, April 1970, pp. 1-7.

——, and Alvin D. Star, "Role of White-Owned Businesses in the Inner City." Working paper, prepared for Inner City Marketing Conference held at State University of Buffalo, June 4-6, 1970.

America, Richard F., Jr., "What Do You People Want?" Harvard Business Review, Vol. 47, March-April 1969, pp. 103-112.

Bauer, Raymond A., Scott M. Cunningham and Lawrence H. Wortzel, "The Marketing Dilemma of Negroes," Journal of Marketing, Vol. 29, July 1965, pp. 1-6.

Bedell, Douglas, "Colored Capitalists," The Wall Street Journal, January 23, 1968.

Binzen, Peter H., "Negro Owned Shopping Center Set to Open with Six White Companies," The Sunday Bulletin, September 15, 1968, p. 1.

"The Birth Pangs of Black Capitalism," Time, Vol. 92 (October 18, 1968), pp. 98-99.

"Black Capitalism, Problems and Prospects," Saturday Review, Vol. 52, August 23, 1969. (Special issue)

"Black Capitalism," The Economist, Vol. 229, December 14, 1968, p. 39.

"Black Capitalism at Work," U.S. News and World Report, February 17, 1969, pp. 60-67.

"Black Capitalism Gets a Test in Pittsburgh," Business Week, October 5, 1968, pp. 56-58.

"Black Capitalism Has a Hollow Ring," Business Week, August 30, 1969, pp. 51-54.

"Black Contractors Sharpen Their Pencils," Engineering News-Record, Vol. 183, July 3, 1969, p. 48.

"Black Ghettos: The American Nightmare," A Symposium, Atlantic, Vol. 129, October 1967, pp. 97-110.

Bloom, Gordon F., "Black Capitalism in Ghetto Supermarkets: Problems and Prospects," Industrial Management Review, Vol. 11, Spring 1970, pp. 37-48.

Bluestone, Barry, "Black Capitalism: The Path to Black Liberation?" The Review of Radical Political Economics, Vol. 1, May 1969, pp. 36-55.

Boggs, James, Charles Johnson, John Williams, "The Myth and Irrationality of Black Capitalism," 2-9 in Proceedings of the National Black Economic Development Conference, Detroit, April 25-27, 1969.

Booms, Bernard H. and James G. Ward, Jr., "The Cons of Black Capitalism—Will This Policy Cure Urban Ills?" Business Horizons, Vol. 12, October 1969, pp. 17-26.

Boone, Louis E. and John A. Bonno, "Food Buying Habits of the Urban Poor," Journal of Retailing, Vol. 47, Fall 1971, pp. 79-84.

Brimmer, Andrew F., "Black Capitalism: An Assessment," paper presented to the 1969 Meeting of the Association for the Study of Negro Life and History, Birmingham, Alabama, October 1969.

——, "The Trouble with Black Capitalism," Nation's Business, Vol. 57, May 1969, pp. 78-79.

——, "Small Business and Economic Development in the Negro Community," pp. 422-437 in "Organization and Operation of the Small Business Administration," Hearing (July 1969) before the Select Committee on Small Business. U.S. House of Representatives, 91st Congress, 1st Session, Washington, D.C., U.S. Government Printing Office, 1969.

——, and Henry S. Terrell, "The Economic Potential of Black Capitalism," Black Politician, Vol. 2, April 1971, pp. 19-23+.

Brouer, Michael and Doyle Little, "White Help for Black Business," Harvard Business Review, Vol. 48, May-June 1970, pp. 4-16; 163-164.

Browne, Robert S., "Barriers to Black Participation in the American Economy," Review of Black Political Economy, Vol. 1, Autumn 1970, pp. 57-67.

Burke, Alice, "Needy Run Own Stores in Boston," Boston Sunday Herald Traveler, April 28, 1968.

"Business Efforts to Aid in Ghetto Missing Goals," Industry Week, Vol. 169, May 17, 1971, pp. 11-12.

"Can Black Run Supers Fill the Inner-City Void?" Progressive Grocer, Vol. 48, April 1969, pp. 190-194.

Chamberlain, John, "Business and Black Capitalism," National Review, Vol. 21, July 29, 1969, pp. 742-744.

Chavis, James M., "Economic Development in the Black Ghetto—A Search for a Workable Model," American Economist, Vol. 14, Fall 1970, pp. 21-25.

"Chicago Leaders Bankroll the Blacks," Business Week, September 13, 1969, p. 56.

"Chrysler Boosts Black Community Development," Iron Age, Vol. 202, December 19, 1968, p. 13.

Cohen, Stanley E., "Business Must Act to Keep Ghetto's Distrust of Crooks from Hurting All," Advertising Age, Vol. 39, April 15, 1968, p. 16.

Conant, Roger R. and James Heilbrun, "Profitability and Size of Firm as Evidence of Dualism in the Black Ghetto," Urban Affairs Quarterly, Vol. 7, March 1972, pp. 251-284.

Conyers, William and Dan Kushner, "The White Jacket in Black Harlem," American Druggist, Vol. 158, October 7, 1968, pp. 15-18.

Cox, William E., "A Commercial Structure Model for Depressed Neighborhoods," Journal of Marketing, Vol. 33, July 1969, pp. 1-9.

DeCoster, Thomas A., "Black Capitalism: Insights into Interviewing," Indiana Business Review, Vol. 46, January-February 1971, pp. 23-26.

"Drive to Set Negroes Up in Business," U.S. News and World Report, Vol. 57, August 31, 1964, p. 82.

DuPree, David, "Harlem-Based Concern Dents a White Preserve, the Construction Field," The Wall Street Journal, November 3, 1969, p. 1.

Eckstein, George, "Black Business—Bleak Business," Nation, Vol. 209, September 15, 1969, pp. 243-245.

Epps, Richard W., "The Appeal of Black Capitalism," Federal Reserve Bank of Philadelphia Business Review, May 1969, pp. 9-15.

Etzel, Michael J., "How Much Does Credit Cost the Small Merchant," Journal of Retailing, Vol. 47, Summer 1971, pp. 52-59.

Farmer, Richard N., "Black Businessmen in Indiana," Indiana Business Review, Vol. 43, November-December 1968, p. 11.

——, "Black Businessmen: Indianapolis," Indiana Business Review, Vol. 45, January-February 1970, pp. 13; 17-20.

——, "Clarification of the Current Situation," Indiana Business Review, Vol. 44, March-April 1969, p. 13.

——, "The Pros of Black Capitalism: A Modest Program Can Pay Dividends," Business Horizons, Vol. 13, February 1970, pp. 37-40.

Fatemi, Ali S.M., "Black Capitalism as a Strategy for Economic Development of the Ghetto," University of Akron Business Review, Vol. 1, Fall 1970, pp. 42-51.

Foley, Eugene P., "The Negro Businessman: In Search of a Tradition," Daedalus, Vol. 95, Winter 1966, pp. 107-144.

Frankenhoff, C.A., "Elements of an Economic Model for Slums in a Developing Economy," Economic Development and Cultural Change, Vol. 16, 1967, pp. 27-35.

Gardner, Charles, "What a Bank Can Do in a Ghetto," Banking, Vol. 64, January 1972, pp. 36-37+.

Garrity, John T., "Red Ink for Ghetto Industries," Harvard Business Review, Vol. 46, May-June 1963, pp. 4-10; 158-161.

Gensen, Dennis H. and Richard Staelin, "The Appeal of Buying Black," Journal of Marketing Research, Vol. 9, May 1972, pp. 141-148.

Gersh, G., "Economic Advances of the American Negro," Contemporary Review, Vol. 207, September 1965, pp. 134-139.

Ginzberg, Eli, "What We Don't Know About the Ghetto," Business Economics, Vol. 4, May 1969, pp. 12-18.

Goodman, Charles S., "Whither the Marketing System in Low-Income Areas," Wharton Quarterly, Spring 1969, pp. 2-10.

Gorkin, S., "Shearson, Hammill and Company and the Ghetto," University of Washington, Business Review, Vol. 29, Autumn 1969, pp. 27-34.

Gross, Paul T., "Problems Facing the Providence Negro Entrepreneur," Rhode Island Business Quarterly, Vol. 4, September 1968, pp. 15-18.

Hall, Mildred and Bill Williams, "The Retailers, the Ghetto and the Government," Merchandising Week, Vol. 99, December 11, 1967, pp. 6-7.

"Harlem Gets Down to Business," Business Week, August 9, 1969, p. 70+.

"Harlem's First Co-op Supermarket Gets Financial Backing from Big Business," Business Week, December 30, 1967, p. 65.

Harrison, Lincoln J., "The Role of the Negro Business School in Promoting Black Capitalism," Journal of Negro Education, Vol. 40, Winter 1971, pp. 45-47.

"He Makes the Ghetto Make Money," Business Week, May 10, 1969, pp. 154-155.

Henderson, William L. and Larry C. Ledebur, "Programs for the Economic Development of the American Negro Community: the Militant Approaches; the Moderate Approach," American Journal of Economics and Sociology, Vol. 29, October 1970, pp. 337-351; Vol. 30, January 1971, pp. 27-45.

——, and Larry C. Ledebur, "The Viable Alternative for Black Economic Developments," Public Policy, Vol. 18, Spring 1970.

"How Students Are Helping Ghetto Businessmen," Management Review, Vol. 58, July 1969, pp. 59-62.

"The Inner City," Food Topics [now Supermarketing], Vol. 22, October 1967, pp. 17-30.

Irons, Edward D., "A Positive View of Black Capitalism," Bankers Magazine, Vol. 153, Spring 1970, pp. 43-47.

"Is Black Capitalism the Answer?" Business Week, August 3, 1968, pp. 60-61.

Johnston, Verle, "Financing the Inner City," Monthly Review of the Federal Reserve Bank of San Francisco, October 1969.

Joyce, George and Norman Govoni, "The Impact of Public Policy on Minority Entrepreneurship: a Relocation Study," Southern Journal of Business, Vol. 5, July 1970, pp. 198-205.

Klein, Richard, "A Synergism: Business Students and the Disadvantaged Entrepreneur," Atlanta Economic Review, Vol. 21, October 1971, pp. 32-35.

Levine, Charles H., "A New Approach," Indiana Business Review, Vol. 44, March-April 1969, p. 12.

Levitan, Sar A. and Robert Taggart III, "Developing Business in the Ghetto," Conference Board Record, Vol. 6, July 1969, pp. 13-21.

London, Paul, "Channeling Business Expertise to Black Entrepreneurs," Management Review, Vol. 58, December 1969, pp. 31-36.

Louviere, Vernon, "Olin Corporation Sows Ghetto 'Seed Money,'" Nation's Business, Vol. 57, December 1969, p. 15.

Loveless, Roland A., "Toward Black Entrepreneurship," American Industrial Development Council Journal, Vol. 5, October 1970, pp. 19-32.

McClelland, David C., "Black Capitalism: Making It Work," Think, Vol. 35, July-August 1969, pp. 6-11.

MacDowell, Harold W. and Louis H. Vorzimer, "Black Capitalism: Opportunity or Myth?" University of Washington Business Review, Vol. 29, Summer 1970, pp. 24-30.

McKersie, Robert B., "Vitalize Black Enterprise," Harvard Business Review, Vol. 46, September-October 1968, pp. 88-89.

McPeak, William, "A Plea for Cooperatives," Inter-racial Review, Vol. 36, November 1963, pp. 215-217.

Mearus, John G., "Cleveland (Changes in the Black Ghetto—II)," Saturday Review, Vol. 53, August 1, 1970, pp. 13-14; 54.

Miller, Kenneth H., "Community Capitalism and the Community Self-Determination Act," Harvard Journal of Legislation, Vol. 6, 1969, pp. 6-11.

Morrill, R.L., "Negro Ghetto: Problems and Alternatives," Geographical Review, Vol. 55, July 1965, pp. 339-361.

Moskowitz, Milton, "Black Capitalism—Where It's At," Business and Society, Vol. 1, December 17, 1968.

Muller, A.L., "Economic Growth and Minorities," American Journal of Economics, Vol. 26, July 1967, pp. 225-230.

"The Negro in Business," Ebony, Vol. 18, September 1963, pp. 211-218.

"Negro Owned and Managed Plant Fills Big Ghetto Need—Jobs," Modern Manufacturing, Vol. 1, September 1968, pp. 80-81.

Pender, David R., "Strategic Hamlets in America . . . An Approach to the Problems of the Urban and Rural Poor," Essays in Economics, September 1969, Columbia, S.C., Vogue Press, 1969.

Petrof, John V., "Customer Strategy for Negro Retailers," Journal of Retailing, Vol. 43, Fall 1967, pp. 30-37.

——, "Negro Entrepreneurship: Myth or Reality?" Marquette Business Review, Vol. 13, Spring 1969, pp. 34-37.

Poinsett, Alex, "The Economics of Liberation," Ebony, Vol. 24, August 1969, pp. 150-154.

"Property Pride Need Spurs Drive for Negro-Owned Stores," Supermarket News, October 17, 1966, p. 23.

Puryear, Alvin N., "Restoration: A Profile of Economic Development," The MBA, Vol. 3, February 1969, pp. 36-40, 48.

"Putting Blacks in the Black," Nation's Business, Vol. 56, December 1968, pp. 58-60.

Rein, Martin, "Social Stability and Black Capitalism," Trans-Action, Vol. 6, June 1969, pp. 4 and 6.

Seldin, Maury and Michael Sumichrast, "Negro Entrepreneurship in the District of Columbia," SBA Economic Review, Spring-Summer 1969, pp. 9-29.

Solo, Robert A., "Business Enterprise and Economic Development," MSU Business Topics, Vol. 15, Winter 1967, pp. 23-29.

Spitz, A.E., "Ghetto Retailing—Entrepreneurial Dilemma," Atlanta Economic Review, Vol. 21, October 1971, pp. 36-37.

Spratlen, Thaddeus H., "Ghetto Economic Development: Content and Character of the Literature," The Review of Black Political Economy, Vol. 1, Summer 1971, pp. 43-71.

Stegner, Wallace, "East Palo Alto (Changes in the Black Ghetto—I)," Saturday Review, Vol. 53, August 1, 1970, pp. 12, 15, 54.

"Stepping Out: Federal Grant Finances Minority Contractors Group," Engineering News-Record, Vol. 181, August 29, 1968, p. 106.

Sturdivant, Frederick D., "Better Deal for Ghetto Shoppers," Harvard Business Review, Vol. 46, March-April 1968, pp. 130-138.

——, "Business and the Mexican-American Community," California Management Review, Vol. 11, Spring 1969, pp. 73-80.

——, "The Limits of Black Capitalism," Harvard Business Review, Vol. 47, January-February 1969, pp. 122-128.

——, and Walter Wilhelm, "Poverty, Minorities and Consumer Exploitation," Social Science Quarterly, Vol. 49, December 1968, pp. 643-650.

Sucsy, Leonard G., "Marketing's New Role in the Ghetto," Sales/ Marketing Today, February 1970, pp. 9-11.

Tabb, William K., "Perspectives on Black Economic Development," Journal of Economic Issues, Vol. 4, December 1970, pp. 68-81.

Taylor, Thayer C., "In the Bigger Cities, Dig Black," Sales Management, Vol. 107, November 15, 1971, p. 71.

Timmons, Jeffry A., "Black Is Beautiful—Is It Bountiful?" Harvard Business Review, Vol. 49, November-December 1971, pp. 81-94.

Tobin, James, "On Improving the Economic Status of the Negro," Daedalus, Vol. 94, Fall 1965, pp. 878-898.

Trosper, Joseph F., "Black Businessmen: Fort Wayne," Indiana Business Review, Vol. 45, January-February 1970, pp. 12; 14-18.

Walter, I. and J. E. Kramer, Jr., "Human Resources and Economic Growth in a Negro Municipality," Business and Government Review (University of Missouri, Columbia), Vol. 9, July-August 1968, pp. 5-17.

Ward, John, "Black Ownership Capitalism in Columbus (Ohio)," Bulletin of Business Research (Ohio State University), Vol. 45, May 1970, pp. 4-8.

"Where Negro Business Gets Credit," Business Week, June 8, 1968, pp. 98-100.

White, Wilford L., "The Negro Entrepreneur," Occupational Outlook Quarterly, Vol. 10, February 1966, pp. 19-22.

"Whites Help Negroes Buy Ghetto Firms as Turmoil Spurs Merchants to Sell Out," Wall Street Journal, August 13, 1968, p. 28.

"Whose Black Capitalism?" The Economist, Vol. 230, March 1, 1969, pp. 39-40.

Williams, J.A., Jr., "The Effects of Urban Renewal Upon a Black Community: Evaluation and Recommendations," Social Science Quarterly, Vol. 50, December 1969, pp. 703-712.

Wolcott, Robert B. and David Nuffer, "Helping an Infant Black Firm," Public Relations Journal, Vol. 25, June 1969, p. 12.

Wright, K.M., "Financing Business in Urban Core Areas," Business Economics, Vol. 4, January 1969, pp. 57-60.

Zeidman, P.F., "Negro Businessmen: Need for Help," An Address, December 8, 1967, Vital Speeches, Vol. 34, January 15, 1968, pp. 209-214.

About the Author

DAVID CAPLOVITZ is currently a professor of sociology at the Graduate Center of the City University of New York. For many years he was a senior research associate of the Bureau of Applied Social Research of Columbia University where he carried out this study. He is the author of *The Poor Pay More* (1963) and *Consumers in Trouble* (1974).

About the Assistants

LOIS SANDERS is completing a doctorate at Columbia University's Teachers College. BERNARD LEVENSON is a professor in the Department of Community Medicine at Mount Sinai School of Medicine. JOAN WILSON is working on her doctorate in the Department of Sociology of New York University.